SEARCH FOR PURPOSE

By ARTHUR E. MORGAN

MY WORLD
   Antioch Press, 1927

PURPOSE AND CIRCUMSTANCE
   Antioch Press, 1928

A COMPENDIUM OF ANTIOCH NOTES
   Antioch Press, 1930

THE SEED MAN
   Antioch Press, 1933

THE LONG ROAD
   National Home Library, 1936 (out of print)

THE SMALL COMMUNITY
   Harper, 1942

EDWARD BELLAMY: A BIOGRAPHY
   Columbia University Press, 1944

THE PHILOSOPHY OF EDWARD BELLAMY
   Kings Crown Press, 1945

NOWHERE WAS SOMEWHERE
   University of North Carolina Press, 1946

A BUSINESS OF MY OWN
   Community Service, Inc., 1946

THE RURAL UNIVERSITY (INDIA)
   Hindustani Talimi Sangh, Sevagram, Wardha, India, 1949

THE MIAMI CONSERVANCY DISTRICT
   McGraw-Hill, 1951

INDUSTRIES FOR SMALL COMMUNITIES
   Community Service, Inc., 1953

SEARCH FOR
PURPOSE

Arthur E. Morgan

THE ANTIOCH PRESS

printed in the
United States of America
by the Antioch Press
Yellow Springs, Ohio

PREFACE

THROUGH THE YEARS I have endeavored to discover and to define valid purpose for my life, and as such purpose has emerged I have tried to examine and test it by whatever data and insight were at my command. This book is an account of that search and of its outcome.

To have a strong popular appeal, a statement of purpose should present a few definite objectives, with the promise that their achievement will bring the kingdom of heaven. I do not have a vision of Utopia. I see problems beyond problems, issues beyond issues, as far as present vision runs. If my outlook is one of aggressive hope, rather than of resignation or of disillusionment, it is because, while I have tried to overlook no doubts, difficulties, or reasons for lack of hope, what I have found gives me an increased sense of value and increased feeling of favorable possibility.

✓   ✓   ✓

In search of a life outlook, the most unideal way would be to expose oneself to but a single kind of evidence, and to be governed by it. An ideal course would be to take into account every possible element of evidence of every kind, and to arrive at the necessary resultant of them all. The best practical approach to such an ideal process is to be aware of the major fields of knowledge and experience, and of kinds of evidence which would have a bearing on the search, and to try not to miss the contribution which may be made by each of them.

But here one finds himself in difficulty, for he enters the domains of the specialists. Within a month, while I was talking with a famous anthropologist, he said: "Laymen should keep out of anthropology. It is a highly specialized field, and for one who has not subjected himself to its rigorous discipline to presume to write or speak concerning its subject matter or its conclusions can only lead to confusion." Similar expressions might seem appropriate in many specialized fields.

The competent specialist disciplines his observations and his reflections, and so in his limited subject develops a "common sense" or intuition that to the average man is a very uncommon sense. On the other hand, one who undertakes to use the data and accepted concepts of many fields in so general a discussion as this concerning life purpose will not have been able to inform, define and discipline his observations and conclusions in all of them, and will surely be vulnerable to criticism by specialists. Even so, his inaccuracies may not be such as to mislead the reader. For instance, the undifferentiated use of the terms "force" and "energy," while unpardonable in a physicist, in such a discussion as this might not mislead any reader or cloud the intended meaning. In case inaccuracies are of such a nature or on such a scale as to falsify a conclusion, that is a different matter.

A person who considers a general problem, such as achieving a life outlook, from the viewpoints of several fields, may have a contribution to make in over-all attitude which the specialist as specialist does not. There are some valid and fairly obvious conclusions which do not become current; first, because the hold of tradition and of the mores is so great that few persons, even among the erudite and mentally disciplined, get free from them to have a first-hand view of life; and second, because many who do achieve such freedom in their own fields do not have the time or the trend of attention to exercise that freedom toward life in general. Effort to express an over-all view should not be given up for fear of criticism by the specialists.

✓   ✓   ✓

When a new element is introduced into an old subject of discussion, the very language may seem foreign and irrelevant, and there is strong probability that the new element will be ignored as an uninteresting intrusion of no real moment. Among philosophers and theologians, the introduction of biological considerations into a search for the possible significance of life is apt to be received in that way.

For a man to understand himself he needs to think of himself as an animal, as well as more than an animal. He cannot think intelligently about himself as an animal unless he is informed as to the nature of biological life. If a man should claim to live without eating physical food we should take him to be a fakir. However, if he presumes to get a sound and representative view of life without a modern biological consideration of himself, he still may be in good repute in some circles.

In my search for purpose for my life I have found it necessary to think of myself as an animal, as well as more than an animal. That means it is necessary sometimes to use the language of biology. If this is an unfamiliar course it is nonetheless necessary. While, therefore, it is suitable to give this explanation of my reason for using biological approaches to various problems, no apology for doing so is in order.

*   *   *

Most serious reading is done for the purpose of confirming the reader's present attitudes. This often is not the case with young people who are in the process of seeking direction and purpose for their lives. If such persons should find this book to be of interest, the author would consider its publication to be justified.

*   *   *

It is customary in the preface of a book to give credit to those who have been consulted in its preparation. To record the names of those with whom I have consulted, or who have read the manuscript from the point of view of their own fields of philosophy, theology, psychology, ethics, anthropology, biology, paleontology, or physics, might be unfair to them as it might imply some degree of responsibility for what I have written. If I thank them anonymously, their reputations for scholarship can remain unimpaired.

A. E. M.

CONTENTS

SEARCH FOR PURPOSE

I   INTRODUCTION

IN THE LONG RUN men give their supreme loyalties to over-all patterns of life, to those ideas and attitudes concerning the nature of the world and of life, which provide them with incentive and direction for living. These patterns of thought and action commonly have gone by the name of religion. Their importance is evidenced by the fact that no human society of any size is long without them, and by the fact that they outlive nations and governments.

Sometimes these patterns remain relatively stable for long periods, with little change except in details, and little disturbance of the main characteristics. At other times, with the growth of experience, insight and outlook, and with great changes of circumstances, the existing patterns cannot contain the new spirit, and there is widespread and deep-seated change.

The present is one of the times of great transition. The world has moved. Through unprecedented growth in communication and interrelations, with ever wider circulation of ideas, through the development of the scientific attitude, especially with the rise of the theory of evolution, with the growth of technology, and with the spread of democratic education, there is much searching for clarification of understanding and incentives. The patterns of life which we have inherited from the ancient past, even as modified through the centuries, are radically inadequate for today.

We have data for thinking and methods of inquiry which the ancient world did not generally possess. It is often said of Christianity, as of their own religions by the followers of other faiths, that its only fault is that it has not been generally applied. That, I believe, is not a sound opinion. There are vast and vital issues pressing on us today concerning which Christian teaching provides no direction.

For instance, there is the problem of population. Take the fundamental principle, all men are brothers.

Our fathers were the first to settle a nearly empty continent, and felt that the general interest justified them in pushing aside primitive people who did not use it intensively. Now, probably more than three hundred millions of our brothers in other lands, crowded in inadequate space, would eagerly welcome an opportunity to come here and share our abundant acres and our modern methods. Since birth rates where they would come from are high, their places at home would soon be filled with an equally dense population, as has been the case in the countries our forefathers left to come to America. Shall we let them come? Are the total values of life greater with our present average of fifty people to the square mile for the country as a whole and three to six hundred in our most populous states, and with space for breathing and for freedom of motion, or is it our duty to our brothers to do unto them as we would have them in similar circumstances do to us, and adopt immigration policies that might result in our soon having a population of several times as many to the square mile, and in the dilution or submergence of our culture? Christian good will alone does not answer that question.

There are numerous issues which are—or should be—in the forefront of the world's thinking which are not dealt with or implied in Christian teaching, or in the teaching of most other great religions. What about eugenics, the scientific attitude, our responsibilities to other life than the human species? What about the disharmonies of religions, each holding that it is the one true faith by which men must be saved; religions which, while having much in common in morals and ethics, are exclusive of each other in their philosophies and theologies, and thus are sources of estrangement and antagonism among men?

The prevailing religious views of life are inadequate. Nor will liberal adaptations, while holding to the central theologies of the old creeds, serve our needs. The world requires new patterns for living, patterns growing in an atmosphere of full freedom from the compulsions of the past, along with concern for the significance of life.

It does not follow that none of the past will be included in the new design. Very much of the past will be kept, some of it with increase of emphasis, not from the compulsion of tradition or authority, but because it survives or emerges in the process of free, objective search. Because not only our own, but all great tradition, will be included in our search, the new patterns will have a richer inheritance from the past than have the old.

As to the process by which the new designs for living will emerge, we have a rough-and-ready, though very inadequate, analogy in the methods which have been used for improving the transmission of the human voice. Through many centuries, good, practical methods were employed to enable speech to carry further. Men practiced to develop large lung capacity and powerful voices. They learned clear and simplified enunciation. They studied acoustics. But now comes a new approach. Men break down the process into its elements. They free themselves from bondage to traditional methods and call upon their knowledge in many fields. And they emerge with new creations whereby a man may speak in an ordinary tone of voice and be heard across the ocean. The good elements of old-time training in enunciation and acoustics are not discarded, but are incorporated in the new. Inventors of the telephone gave up all feeling of need for loyalty to the over-all pattern of traditional ways for transmitting the human voice, yet at every step they used the values of old-time knowledge, not only of linguistics, but also in a thousand skills, some of them as mechanical as the arts of drawing wire.

This analogy somewhat illustrates the process of reducing a problem to its elements and of building with those elements without regard for likeness or unlikeness to traditional pat-

5

terns. In this process something new has been added to the prospects of the human adventure.

In the vast propaganda of the present day, three kinds of servitude are pressed upon men. One of these is to traditional religious beliefs and attitudes. The second is servitude to custom. The third servitude is to man's animal impulses. A person who keeps himself free from all these servitudes may seem to his associates to be alien and a menace. Yet freedom from them helps the search for a way of life.

A pattern of thought and action which is adequate for the present time will not appear suddenly and fully matured. It must be a gradual growth, contributed to by many men. If there is communication among such persons they may profit by each other's experience, reflection and insight.

While I was still a boy I became imbued with the idea that nothing was more important than that I should get general direction, purpose and motivation for my life. In my efforts to that end I was under great pressure, on the one hand to accept without question the conventional religious beliefs in which I grew up; and on the other hand to dismiss all such elements of my cultural tradition as obsolete and not worth consideration. From then until the present this matter of achieving over-all purpose and direction has been a primary concern—though by no means calling for a major part of my total time and attention. Plans for the journey of life are not made primarily for the pleasure of planning, but in the interest of a successful journey. Unless one uses his plans for actual traveling, his planning has no more value than does playing chess. In this present effort to tell how I went about the undertaking to find purpose and motivation for my life, and of the results, I had the possibility in mind that some other persons might be saved some of the stresses I experienced, and might be helped in their own process of inquiry, and perhaps strengthened in their motives.

6

II MY PERSONAL APPROACH

DURING MY EARLY YEARS, especially from the time I was about fourteen until my early twenties, I made intense and sustained efforts to achieve a view of life that would be *in accord with what is,* and that would provide design and incentive for living. I found few among my personal associates of that time who made such sustained effort. Some of them uncritically accepted the prevailing religious pattern, while some were indifferent or hostile to such concerns. The loyalties of some of those who were my associates by circumstance were to their animal impulses or to other rudimentary interests. This was especially true of the members of labor gangs in which I worked in my 'teens. Of sustained, objective inquiry I found very little in my local environments.

My father had given up all religious affiliation and belief, and was inclined to be objective and reflective. Yet he so seldom expressed his views that I can only conjecture his personal beliefs from occasional remarks. I judge that he had dismissed theology and ontology as speculation not based on evidence, and priests and ministers as either naive or exploiters. His reading was limited, but not trivial. He knew much of Shakespeare by heart, and his selections were excellent. He read Burns a great deal. I recall when very young thinking how trivial was his interest in being enamored of Burns' fine poem, "To a Mouse." He read science and mathematics, and had an amateur chemistry laboratory in the house.

However, my father seemed lazy, untidy, procrastinating, a poor provider for his family. Until later I did not recognize the modesty and dignity of his character. My mother, though frail in body, carried most of the household drudgery, managed on extremely little money, and bore the brunt of Father's criticism. She was orthodox, sincerely and intensely re-

7

ligious, and always helpful to friends and neighbors. She provided much of the family income by keeping student boarders. She sincerely indoctrinated me in her beliefs and moral principles, and I took on the pattern of these beliefs and attitudes. I resented my father's failure to carry his share of the family burden, and his criticism, and was a strong partisan of my mother. I did not think of myself as being influenced by my father, but probably I was. I have greatly appreciated the fact that, though there was marked difference of personality and outlook between them, there was no doubt in the mind of either that our home was a permanent and stable institution.

By the age of nine I had acquired a strong purpose to commit myself without reserve to achieving a good way of life, which at that time I took to be the pattern of belief and conduct of the evangelical Protestant church in which I was growing up. When I was about ten I was baptized by immersion into membership in the local Baptist church, the youngest member by several years. Our pastor and my mother strongly approved this action; my father disapproved, but made no objection.

At that age my natural curiosity ranged far and wide. When the circus came to town I would recognize every animal in the cages from having read about them in the *Woods' Natural History* which my mother had given me. Through Father's acquaintance with them I knew most of the trees, and with Mother's help a large part of the wild flowers, within two miles from our home. On the streets of our town I intensively observed men and women of various social and economic levels, and where possible overheard their conversations, to see whether any class seemed to have more than the average amount of happiness. In our frontier town, new found wealth, largely from lumbering and from land sales, or from the law, seems to have gone rather hard with its possessors, largely through personal dissipation. Therefore it took little acumen for me to conclude that material wealth has little ne-

8

cessary relation to happiness. Perhaps those observations had something to do with the fact that accumulation of financial resources never has been my primary interest.

In the course of my general curiosity, by the time I was eight I was turning over in my mind some of the theological phrases I heard at church. For instance, I was taught that God is all-powerful, that there is nothing he cannot do. Suppose, I would say to myself, that there has been a certain occurrence, say, that I have been born. Could God make it that that never had taken place? Whatever he did, would not the fact remain? If so, then there was something he could not do. Even while playing games with schoolmates or with neighbor children such childish speculations would be running through my mind.

I enjoyed playmates, but also was not averse to solitude. My tolerance, and later my liking for it, may have resulted partly from the fact that while I loved the woods and the rivers, I could scarcely find a boy to share that interest with me, except for hunting or trapping, and so I frequently went alone. With periods of solitude came undisturbed opportunity to turn over in my mind problems which arose from my reading and from my associations and experiences.

Our little town library was an exceptionally fine collection of the world's great literature, donated through a curious circumstance by the great Edward Everett. This was a precious window onto life and thought, especially in science and philosophy. Through some influence I never learned, the books on science had been kept fairly well up to date. This library was like foster parents to me. So far as I could find, there were few persons among my schoolmates and associates who had thought critically enough about the purposes and problems of life to ask very pertinent questions. My father might have been a helpful companion, but it never occurred to me to open my mind to him until I began to work with him in my twenties, and even then only to a very limited extent. The library was a whole congregation of friends. Some

9

of the authors were asking themselves just the questions I was asking myself. There and from similar sources during the next few years I found writings which moved me very deeply. In addition to books on science there were such standard works as Carlyle's *Sartor Resartus*, Ruskin's *Unto This Last*, Tolstoi's *My Confession*, Wordsworth's *Prelude*, Tennyson's *In Memoriam*, and Sidney Lanier's poems, along with Bacon, Montaigne, Epictetus, Emerson and Thoreau. Also, I read many less known authors. It was not only the thoughts these men expressed which appealed to me, but the climate in which they lived.

When I was perhaps sixteen years old I read Henry Drummond's *The Ascent of Man*, a discussion of evolution. As I recall, this was a mild, semireligious book, but the concept of evolution which it presented struck me with great force. I had heard of evolution as a vague theory, but never had understood what it involved. The concept seemed to answer a host of questions, and seemed to make somewhat understandable a world that theretofore had been in some respects a meaningless jumble. It was as though I had come out of a dark cave into the light. Observing biological relationships and seeing evidences of organic evolution became an absorbing occupation. (Though my formal study of biology was limited to about five months in high school when I was sixteen or seventeen, and to about six weeks when I was nineteen, my interest and reading in the subject has continued intermittently to the present.)

With the leaders of the church congregation of which I was a member the doctrine of evolution was held to be false, a temptation which might lead me astray. That attitude posed a clean-cut question: is it right to inquire, or should one suppress his inquiry to maintain his faith? For probably a year or more I struggled with this question, an effort made more intense by my determination to commit myself unreservedly to a good way of life. My well-trained high school teacher in biology, I believe only one teaching generation removed

10

from Agassiz, had the same conflict. He quit his teaching career to continue a good Methodist, and went to selling life insurance. Never in the more than sixty years since then have I applied myself more intensively and unremittingly, or with more complete sincerity, to any question. My religious advisers, sincere people whose personal lives and character I respected, strongly urged that I hold to the faith.

A local circumstance complicated the situation for me. Our own small orthodox congregation was made up mostly of honest, friendly, hard-working people. The liberal (Unitarian) church in the town had a few conspicuous members I did not respect. One of them was president and owner of our principal bank. His bank failed, and many persons of small means lost their life savings. Two or three years later this man built for himself what to our town was a palatial home. One or two other members of that church had similar personal standards. They were the only members of the congregation I knew anything about. I did not know until years later how far such persons were from being representative Unitarians. My mother, whose acquaintance with that denomination went little further than mine, would point to these men, and then to our own honest, hard-working members and say, "By their fruits ye shall know them."

In the face of this practical, pragmatic evidence it was more difficult for me to decide that nevertheless I must choose the way of free inquiry. It was reasonable for me to ask myself, "Is there here some inherent relation between cause and effect which I do not understand, but which I had better not ignore?" Nevertheless I came to the conclusion that I could not take that evidence as representative or conclusive, and I decided for free inquiry. This was in 1894.

A year or two later I had practical support for my conclusion. When I reached high school I found the principal, a tall, rugged Vermont woman of complete integrity, vigorous intelligence and common sense, was a member of the Unitarian church. Her character helped give me assurance of the

11

reasonableness of the course I already had taken. Until many years later I never discussed religion with her. It was how she conducted herself from day to day, and the straightness of her mind, that impressed me.

When I was fifteen I listened to a Buddhist, a Dr. Dhammapala of Ceylon (who for nearly half a century afterwards was probably the foremost Buddhist in southeast Asia). I was deeply impressed by his intelligence, his apparent sincerity, and his personality. This was my first contact with marked quality from outside the part of the world called Christian.

As I asked myself, "Why do people believe?" it became clear that religious beliefs have varied reasons or causes. One of the chief causes is that men and women grow up among people who believe. It appeared that of all Moslems in the world probably more than 95% are sons or daughters of Moslems; of all Christians in the world, probably more than 95% are children of Christians; and so with Buddhists, Hindus and others. Moreover, each great religious leader had been conditioned by his own religious and cultural background. Jesus' teaching clearly reflects the teachings of the Hebrew prophets and of his close Galilean neighbors, the Stoics. Similarly, Buddha's teachings have much of the character of the Hindu world in which he lived.

By and large, though with many individual exceptions, each of the devotees of each religion believes his is the one true faith which justifies his full acceptance. Yet, so far as theology and theories of the nature of the world are concerned, there are great differences. For instance, the Christian and the Hindu ideas of what happens after death are strikingly different. Not all these varying beliefs can be true.

As to a large part of the world's population, each person lives in a religious atmosphere of his own kind, where the influences that mold him, the teaching, the example, nearly all are those of a certain faith. These influences, often without his being conscious of the fact, fix his "second nature." It is significant that the people of each faith have the same deep

12

inner feeling as the people of other faiths do that they have the very truth. If a devout, orthodox Christian wants to know how a devout, orthodox Moslem feels about the Moslem faith he needs only to look within himself and to note his own deep inner sense of having the true faith. The Moslem has the same deep inner sense of assurance about *his* faith. (I have been interested when going among Moslems in later years to observe the intensity and completeness of that inner assurance. It seems to me to go far beyond that which most Christians have, doubtless because the Moslem bringing up has been less influenced by the literature of free inquiry and by other diverse outlooks.)

The confirmed, orthodox follower of each faith has been taught that his inner sense of assurance is conclusive evidence of the truth of his beliefs. He has been taught from childhood to trust it so long as it accords with the accepted beliefs of his religion. Yet that deep, inner sense of assurance of having the true faith can be, and is, induced in people with reference to almost any belief, especially if the influence is exerted in early life.

From the time I was sixteen years old such observations came to take fairly definite form. The shelves of our town library provided more encouragement for such thinking than did my personal associates.

III THE PROCESS OF INQUIRY

IT WAS from such observations and from my reflection that I came to ask myself the question, "How do I know that the particular faith in which I was born and reared is the one true faith?" I asked myself, "What shall I believe?" and then went on to the further question, "Why should I believe?" What is the validity of the feeling with which I have grown up, that it is very important to have a belief?

Perhaps the most difficult decision I ever made was that my own deep conditioning should be examined. When I did arrive at that conclusion I went far beyond the immediate issue. I arrived at the conclusion that free, critical inquiry is more than a right—it is a duty. I concluded, also, that inquiry cannot be free so long as there is an emotional drag holding one to particular beliefs. Desire or intent to justify a particular belief or attitude leads to unrepresentative selection and inaccurate weighing of evidence. It would be my aim not to try to make myself believe any doctrine or theory, nor to try not to believe. I would want my beliefs and opinions to be my best judgment from the evidence, not adopted because of comfort or courage I would get from believing. If I should be convinced that for me to know the truth, or to give up some current belief by finding it untrue, would take away my comfort and remove the present basis for my hope, nevertheless, I should seek to know the truth.

In determining what to believe I would try to look at the beliefs in which I grew up in the same way in which I would look at the other beliefs in which other people had grown up. I would look at my own inner sense of assurance critically, from the outside, as I would look at the inner sense of assurance of a person of "alien" faith. I would look at its sources, the circumstances of its origin, and its characteristics. I would ask myself, not "How can I justify and strength-

14

en the beliefs, attitudes and doctrines I have come by?" but "Are they the most reasonable beliefs?"

I do not want to hold any belief because it is perhaps true or probably true. If something is perhaps true I would think of it as possibility; if it is probably true I would think of it as probability. If I have no reasonably conclusive evidence for or against something being true I prefer to say—and think— I do not know.

We inquire only where we doubt. If I adopt a certain belief because of the comfort or courage it gives me, then, as to the matter involved in that belief my mind is at rest and ceases to inquire. A mistaken belief, therefore, is an effective barrier against the search for truth. (I do not think of the truth as some absolute existence, but as in contrast to what is untrue. "Truth" might be defined as any part, or the total, of all truths.) As to any issue, the attitude of search and of inquiry is more apt to throw light on the subject than does the attitude of having already settled the matter.

Also, when we have committed ourselves to a conclusion we are likely to be partisans of that conclusion and to seek to sustain it by emotional commitment to it. Philosophers and theologians, like most other people, are inclined to cast their lot with some doctrine or system of thought, and afterwards to become partisan defenders of that doctrine rather than real inquirers concerning it. In my opinion the attitude of suspended judgment, where the evidence is not reasonably conclusive, is practically productive, as well as philosophically sound. A critical, inquiring attitude seems to me to be a fundamental ethical obligation. Any surrender to credulity or to wishful thinking is treason to our desire to find or to create significance.

That does not by any means prevent me from having a "working hypothesis." If I am trying to go to town and am not sure of the way, an attitude of suspended judgment and continued inquiry does not prevent my traveling vigorously in the most probable direction. I may make most headway, and

15

throw more light on the problem, by traveling than by standing still.

Effort to avoid wishful thinking need not result in a lessening of hope and expectation. In fact, determination to avoid wishful thinking is evidence of hope and of something very much akin to faith. Unless one has hope and expectation he will not have incentive to avoid wishful thinking. Inquiry to find whether life is significant, or can be made so, with a strong desire to find that it can be, is justified and is highly desirable, but the desired end probably will not be furthered by credulity. At its best, desire to find that life is significant or can be made so will be more than an exploration to find what *is*. It will be a creative effort to find out what might be, and may be a determining factor in the emergence of significance.

At a time when men could not travel by air, critical inquiry to find whether flying is possible was properly motivated by a strong desire to find flying to be possible. But that very desire called for critical, rigorous, objective thinking. Wishful thinking probably would defeat its purpose. The Wright brothers, in their invention of the airplane, were not simply inquirers to find out whether flying is theoretically possible. They were creators to devise an unprecedented organization of matter and energy which would make flying feasible. They were not less scientific because they hoped and desired to find flying to be feasible. Their very desire impelled them to critical scientific objectivity. Their purpose and desire were among the determining causes of great events. I know that their inquiring attitude extended to every field of thinking.

✓   ✓   ✓

It seemed to me that sometimes subjects remain active issues long after they might have been settled, because we feel it to be necessary or virtuous to search for reasons for continuing traditional beliefs and attitudes, rather than to inquire without predilection as to whether the beliefs are inherently

16

reasonable. Especially in the religious field one finds that to be the case.

In reading the lives of martyrs it is noticeable that seldom did one of them possess or seem to crave full freedom to inquire. Usually they departed from conventional beliefs only in certain limited particulars. Thomas More authorized the execution of heretics whose heresy consisted in insistence on reading the catechism to their children in English, rather than in Latin. While that case may be extreme, it is somewhat typical. Most martyrs loudly proclaimed their loyalty to the main body of prevailing doctrine. Giordono Bruno was an exception. His seemed to be a free mind.

Very generally in the liberal religious field there is the attitude, "Of course we hold to the common fundamentals of the Christian doctrine. It is only the false accretions and adulterations which we repudiate." Commonly there is lack of courage or inclination to say, "Why should we accept them?" and to follow through without predilection to find an answer. Too often the question we ask ourselves is not, "Is this true?" but rather, "What evidence can we gather to enable us to continue to hold this belief?" That attitude is not true inquiry, but is flight from inquiry.

In religion, politics and other fields this is the prevailing course. As I have lived or moved among deeply religious people—Catholic, Protestant, Mormon, Moslem, Hindu—and have seen deep sincerity of life and a fine sense of human brotherhood, it has seemed tragic that those fine qualities should be associated with mythological doctrines which serve as barriers, and that often these people have been taught to give greater weight to their mythologies than to the fine human qualities of which they have so much in common.

It sometimes seems that the less evidence there is for a belief, or the more unreasonable or improbable it is, the greater the intensity with which it is pressed upon us. For such beliefs a strong emotional charge is built up. We are

17

made to feel that it is right to believe, and wrong not to believe. This emotional state makes real inquiry difficult. The religious and social atmosphere becomes so charged with feeling that anyone who does not conform in his beliefs is looked upon as a questionable character. Fear of doubting reduces real inquiry and the progress in understanding of which men are capable.

Full freedom of inquiry does not call for uncritical disregard for prevailing beliefs. If a belief has been held by a large number of people through a long period there is a natural presumption that it has inherent worth. It would be arbitrary and uncritical to dismiss such beliefs as though they were not worth examination. In my own case, when I had decided on a course of free inquiry I did not at once separate myself from my religious associates. They were largely persons of sincerity and good will, and I felt that their social and ethical attitudes had much value. For several years I continued fairly active in church affairs, especially in doing voluntary janitor work and in general in trying to make myself practically useful. My separation from earlier beliefs and associations was gradual, taking place through several years as somewhat deliberately formed judgment dictated. But because of the deliberateness of that process, the separateness which resulted was the more complete. It was not just emotional revolt.

The problem of authority in beliefs and opinions is not the simple one of declaring one's independence. The accumulated experience, insight and judgment of men largely makes up the fabric of civilization. How to maintain full freedom of inquiry, and yet to preserve the values of our cultural inheritance, remained as a continuing problem. So with myself it was no longer a matter of loyalty or disloyalty to absolute or revealed truth, but was resolved into practical questions of experience, insight, inquiry and judgment in particular areas or cases. My inquiries tended to erase some of the sharp lines between true and false, good and bad, right and

18

wrong, and to replace them with judgments of more or less probable or of better or worse.

In some ways my reading complicated my inquiries. When I read specifically antireligious books such as *The Conflict of Religion and Science*, by the chemist, Draper, I was repelled by their prejudice and venom; and when I read apologies for religion, such as Butler's *Analogies*, I was disappointed by their uncritical thinking. Most of what fell into my hands to read seemed so lacking in truly critical inquiry as to incline me to the opposite point of view. I would say to myself, "Is that all the foundation they have for their positions?" As I listened to political speakers, the absence of impartial inquiry was further emphasized. Was it not possible, I asked myself, to approach important questions without predilection or prejudice? I determined that I would try to achieve that attitude.

My Self-Assurance Is Limited. When I was nine or ten years old my mind and spirit were committed to living the best I know, regardless of the cost to me. Since I was about sixteen I have been committed to complete freedom of inquiry, regardless of what effect that would have on my beliefs, outlook or hope. (My idea of complete freedom of inquiry has not involved taking serious risks without counting the cost, such as becoming addicted to opium to find out what that would be like.)

Why has such commitment had no more significant results in my own life? There are several reasons. First has been my own mediocre and limited personality in motive, intelligence, energy, vitality, education and judgment. But aside from weakness of will, cowardice, and selfishness, which interfered with my living up to my purposes, there was another reason for hesitation to commit myself unreservedly to a course which seemed to me right. This was a feeling that my wisdom and judgment, and my personal stability, were not adequate to justify or to sustain extreme action.

I saw well-meaning, sometimes very intelligent, men whose judgment was erratic, or who were keenly sensitive to some elements of experience, but blind to others. I saw many social, religious and political movements in which commitment and enthusiasm had outrun wisdom and judgment, sometimes with a great waste of human resources. I did not want to be a cause of such waste. A given level and balance of intelligence and a given stability of temperament and of constitution will safely sustain a given intensity of purpose and commitment and a given degree of self-assurance, just as a steam boiler of given material and construction will safely withstand steam pressure only to a certain limit. I saw persons whose intense singlemindedness had carried them to mental or emotional warps, or to acceptance of supposed absolutes where all that the data justified was relative judgment of probabilities of truth or error, of right or wrong or of better or worse.

I felt, too, that in my case much isolation from people would not be good for the development of judgment and wisdom, and that too variant a course would tend to greater isolation. In my earlier years I had spent much time by myself, commonly in association with "nature." I had received great benefit from this course, but came to feel that a greater degree of human association would be beneficial. Also, isolation would be begging the question. I believed that in most cases a good life should be lived through the necessary process of making a living, having a family, and maintaining normal social relations.

In the process of making a living I tended to take on the habits, attitudes and incentives of my associates. In an effort to get an economic foothold in an engineering practice without the benefit of formal engineering schooling or apprenticeship to trained and experienced engineers, and with poor

20

physical health, I felt the pressure of economic necessity. In my intense effort to prove to myself that I could survive economically, my attention for several years was chiefly on my daily work. That course seemed desirable and necessary, not only for economic survival, but for achieving balance and proportion of personality.

This effort to share in the life around me while maintaining my own standards had the result that sometimes the clarity of my convictions and the consistency of my actions were marred. I do not regret having shared rather fully to the degree I did in the current activities of my time. It was better, I think, to fail sometimes to live by my convictions than to hide myself in inaction or in a sheltered position where I would be supported by the labor of men who did meet the everyday exigencies of common life.

Moreover, I found that I needed experience as a basis for judgment. Some men may have such clear insight and such sure powers of generalization that they can generalize truly from a very small basis of experience. I have to learn largely from experience. My powers of generalization are so limited that commonly I need a broad base of experience for the discipline and correction of such generalizations as I may make.

Even during the period when I was struggling to get an economic foothold I was not unmindful of the standards I had set for myself. For instance, it was my desire not to become a person of privilege, but to share the common lot of men. Perhaps there was more reliance then than now on friendly influence and on the favor of one's own group. In my home community, successful men who were not Roman Catholics (who were said to turn business to each other) commonly were members of the Masonic order. It was repeatedly pointed out to me by my Masonic friends that Masons stood by each other, that not being a Mason was almost a reason for disrepute, and that in not being a member of the order I was cutting myself off from a major source of support and benefit. However, such membership seemed to me to be the way to a certain privilege of position. I wanted to share the common lot of the unprivileged, and never joined the Masons.

Before long my income was somewhat higher than that of ordinary workers. I lived very economically, and until past thirty used any surplus for whatever purposes seemed to me worth while, making very modest contributions to various interests, keeping for myself only enough to meet my working needs for a few months. At about that time I married into a Quaker family which had a habit of simple, adequate living, thrift, and the accumulation of modest resources, and that became our family pattern. Also as my work took on larger dimensions money became a necessary tool, and I began to accumulate moderate reserves. Those savings are now small in relation to the funds I have administered and the responsibilities I have carried, but they are larger than those of the normally thrifty working man. I cannot say that I have lived up to the purpose of sharing the lot of the unprivileged, and I have somewhat justified my course by asking myself whether there are not some types of usefulness which preclude complete sharing.

✓   ✓   ✓

People from whose standards I differed were perhaps as sure of theirs as I was of mine. What reason had I to think that my convictions were nearer right than theirs? In working with other people on common undertakings I sometimes went part way in working by group standards, rather than by my own, not necessarily from self-interest or cowardice, but because I had not full assurance of being right. When differences became such that the group was acting by standards or motives that are clearly repudiated by the general judgment of the ethical leaders of mankind, and sometimes otherwise when my own convictions were strong, I could clearly and without misgivings hold to my own convictions, even against dominant group judgment.

I used to read how such men as John Woolman and George Fox had complete assurance of being directed by God, and of their resulting complete confidence of being right, even when alone. I did not feel that I had reason for such confidence that I was right. In some cases where I had with much effort arrived at a clear judgment I felt justified in holding to it, even if I seemed to be nearly alone. One such case was my conviction that I must have a free mind. I did not find general support for that attitude. I distrusted any feeling of having had the truth revealed to me.

Such uncertainty as to judgment and temperamental stability is apt to develop into an excuse for doing the convenient thing, rather than the right thing. I have tried to avoid that, though not with complete success. As I look back I see cases where my personal convictions were followed more rigorously than my present judgment would justify. In other cases I unwisely allowed the action I would have taken in acting according to my own judgment to be overruled by emotions or by the judgment of my associates. Considering my limitations of judgment and of personal ability, I believe that my general attitude of not always having sure confidence in my own judgment, or in the validity of my convictions, has been sound. I do not have a feeling that I would have had sure protection from error if I had had complete confidence in my convictions, or in "divine guidance." Some of my close friends believe that this lack has greatly limited my life.

Without doubt some men much undervalue their own judgment, while others greatly overvalue theirs. I believe that some men have a temperament of great confidence in their own judgment which has little relation to their real judgment and wisdom. Yet the world largely accepts a man's judgment of himself, if it is strongly and skillfully expressed. Even more, a person who expresses doubts of his own judgment

23

will seldom find the current world having great confidence in him. Very often people crave oracles rather than fellow searchers for the truth.

Through the years my process of inquiry, along with other influences and experiences, has led to a number of convictions and opinions, some of them on matters of present-day interest, others on issues which, though now in eclipse, have been of deep concern to men through the ages. While I consider all my conclusions to be tentative, in that they are subject to new evidence, yet as to some of them I have arrived at such strong feeling of certainty that they would not be easily disturbed, and I am ready to commit my life to them. In other words, I might be considered "a person of strong convictions." Through the years those convictions have come to cover a considerable part of the area of thought and action.

Every living thing seems to have a "faith" or inner hope and expectation which motivates effort to fulfill its possibilities. In man that innate biological faith underlies all doctrines, beliefs, philosophies and theories. Yet, reflective man is not satisfied with that biological faith. He wants to examine it, to justify it and to direct and strengthen it. These efforts define his religion.

It has been my aim not to encourage my biological faith by uncritically accepting beliefs. Rather, I would question without limit. My sense of assurance, if any, would be such as would survive that process. The sense of assurance which emerges, I find, seems more substantial and less vulnerable than that with which I started to inquire. The total of those matters on which I have come to have a feeling of strong, though tentative, conviction tends to support and strengthen the biological faith which all men have in some degree whether they recognize it or not, and together they constitute the faith I live by.

However, there are many issues, some of them very important, on which I do not see clearly. On some highly im-

24

portant questions I do not take a clear stand because I do not know what stand to take.

For instance, I feel uncertain as to whether war, as it is practiced and as it surely would be practiced, is ever justified. I do not mean that I hesitate to express my convictions, but rather that my convictions are not clear. I do feel certain that search for possible preferable alternatives commonly is neglected. A more widespread and active doubt as to the efficacy of war to settle questions surely would lead to deeply concerned and active search for better methods. If war should not be entirely eliminated by such search, its occurrence probably would be greatly reduced. I use this issue of war simply to illustrate the fact that there are very important issues on which I am uncertain.

This case also illustrates the fact that uncertainty does not necessarily lead to inaction. My uncertainty drives me to feel the need for active, vigorous search for a course of action which will make this question an academic, rather than a practical one. There are unexplored alternatives to war.

There are other questions which, at least at present, are inherently unanswerable. No one has been able to conclusively prove or disprove the doctrine of Platonic idealism; however, it seems that a desirable way of life would be the same, whichever answer is true. There are varied and conflicting assertions of orthodox Christianity and of other religions, especially as to specific conditions of life after death, for which I see no evidence excepting conflicting claims of divine revelation. If I should assert that it has been revealed to me that there are planets in the constellation Orion where human spirits reside after death, no one could prove me wrong. I do not concern myself with these varied and conflicting assertions.

What Is Religion. By my religion I mean those aspirations, convictions, disciplines, beliefs and motives that actually give direction and character to my life. Sometimes these

25

elements are called religion, sometimes not. Seeking a religion that would result in my best realizing my possibilities in the interest, not primary of myself personally, but of all life, present and future, has, I think, been my first interest through the years. I have wanted to discover what the realities of my situation are, what are the possibilities, and where the values or possibility of values lie, and I have desired optimum motivation for realizing those possibilities. Through the years, as the major outlines of my religion have become stabilized, the thought and attention given to forming beliefs and opinions has grown less, though increase of experience continues to bring change. The need for thought and effort to give effect to my convictions has not decreased in like proportion. While I have not nearly lived up to my religion, it has largely defined my aims, and has influenced my actions.

The Need for Patience. One of my early conclusions was largely effective in relieving me from excessive stress of inquiry. In my early searching for a faith to live by I had an anxious feeling that I must soon find the truth or life would not be worth living. I soon came to realize that this is an unintelligent position. Should a five-year-old child take that attitude, no stress of effort would overcome his immaturity. As to some problems we face we are like five-year-old children; no intensity of effort on our part would quickly bring understanding. Active inquiry to the limits of our powers should be associated with patience to await maturity. As to some issues, that may mean many generations. I believe that I can increasingly develop good judgment as to the direction in which to travel.

The Place of Authority. If I am committed to full and free inquiry, then what is the place of authority? When we try to discover the world for ourselves we may make unnecessary mistakes. When I was about fifteen years old, a

26

schoolmate had a little chemistry laboratory in which he and I worked together. While we knew very little chemistry, we were not relying greatly on authority, but were finding things out at first hand for ourselves. We once boiled away some mercury in our little room, and got some of it in our lungs. That was serious. We survived by good luck, rather than by good sense. It would have been better for us to be more aware of authority in the field of chemistry, and to have known when to rely on it.

One frequently meets the problem of authority in practical life, sometimes where it is a matter of life and death. It is not feasible for us personally to experience and to test all those things we come upon that are not good for us. It is the part of wisdom to learn when not to undertake to find out by personal experience, but to act on authority.

This principle holds true in the field of morals and ethics. It takes less mental acumen to see the need for authority where ignoring it may bring sudden death than where its lack may only gradually debase character or infringe on the welfare of others, but the need for authority is not measured by the difficulty of recognizing it. In ethics, as in most other phases of living, there is need for recognizing authority. (By authority I do not mean power to wield a club, but the position of having achieved sound and informed judgment.) There is need to recognize, in ethics as elsewhere, that we in our generation did not begin the world, that it started some time before we came, that there have been people of more than ordinary foresight and insight, and that for us to take their judgment into account is wise.

A practical respect for authority can go along with a free spirit. I conclude from authority and not from personal experience that it is not well to develop the habit of taking opium. I have not found out by personal experience what the habit would do to me, how it would take away my ability to handle myself, would destroy my power to resist it, would

27

disintegrate my personality and wreck my life; but there is so much reliable evidence to that effect that those who have that evidence speak with authority, which I do well to respect. I do not believe what I have heard about opium because of what some self-interested or closed-minded person told me. I can go beyond that to the considered judgment of those who through competent observation of opium users are in a position to know. If I happen to live in a social atmosphere where taking opium is customary, and where I am under pressure to follow that custom, my resistance to that pressure is ethical conduct, not the less if I clearly understand the effects of the habit. Ethical action often consists of making one's actual behavior conform to what he very well knows is the better course.

We often hear it said in substance concerning the field of ethics and morals, "Since ethical counsel is conflicting and confusing, the only reasonable course left me is to go my own way and to arrive at my own conclusions." That, I think, is an attitude of ignorance. If a person with no knowledge of physics should hear a discussion by physicists in which there was wide difference of opinion it might well appear to him that since so-called authorities disagree, one man's opinion in the field of physics is as good as another's. Only by having some degree of competence can one distinguish between chemistry and alchemy, or between astronomy and astrology, or between ignorance and competence in physics. Only if a person has qualified himself to have opinions on morals and ethics will he see that one man's opinion is not as good as another's.

Widespread acceptance of a course of conduct does not give it ethical authority. When half our nation was keeping slaves, that did not make human slavery an ethical practice. The practice of a powerful religious hierarchy in trying to close the mind of youth to other outlooks by putting books on an index of forbidden literature, by prohibiting attendance at meetings where other outlooks are presented, and by trying

28

to atrophy the attitude of critical inquiry—the widespreadness of such practice does not give it ethical authority, but only the power of strategy.

Reverence or respect for deeply imbedded opinion is by no means a sure guide. I once had an experience which illustrates that fact. One of my early surveying commissions when I was in my mid-twenties was an order from a district court in Minnesota to divide the level bed of an old lake among the owners whose properties bordered the old shore line. When I searched for a legal basis for such an apportioning I found a curious condition. In the case of dried-up lakes, where the length is not markedly greater than the width, the well established legal rule was that in apportioning the lake bed to the owners around the shore, straight lines should be drawn to the center of the lake bed from wherever the property lines intersected the shore line. That is, each owner along the shore would receive a part of the lake bed shaped like a piece of pie, all the pieces meeting at the center of the lake bed.

Now, this would be a good rule if the lake shore were a perfect circle or a regular polygon. However, almost no lake is so symmetrical. Usually it has the shape of an irregular polygon, and an irregular polygon has no center. After trying all sorts of expedients such as finding the center of the largest inscribed circle, the smallest circumscribed circle, etc., and finding none of them even nearly suitable, I followed back the legal decisions in similar cases as far as they went in America, and then to England, but nowhere was there evidence that this obvious absurdity had occurred to the courts. The impossible doctrine had gone down through the centuries, probably applied in each case by a practical surveyor who did not choose to trouble the court with mathematical theory. The judge for whom I executed the order was a frontier man, a narrowly educated, legalistic person who, I thought, could never be made to think that a self-educated rustic of about twenty-four could disclose an error in all the line of judicial decisions on the subject in the great courts of America and England.

I made the best allocation I could, and reported to the court. When the court asked how I had determined the center of the lake bed I replied, "Oh, I took the geographical center," and his legal mind was satisfied.[1]

Our great cultural tradition is a mixture of the true and the false, of the important and the trivial, the timely and the obsolescent, the universal and the local or casual. It is vision and wisdom, mixed with myth and speculative abstraction. Such a mixed inheritance should neither be uncritically embraced nor carelessly discarded. When an ore smelter reduces a ton of ore to get a half-ounce of gold no easy-going or hit-or-miss process is followed. Disciplined care and thoroughness are necessary to prevent loss and to get the full value. Yet that may be the best available way to get gold. So it is with our ethical, religious and cultural inheritance. Determination of what we shall keep and what we shall eliminate requires both trained, discriminating intelligence and disciplined motive. It is the part of wisdom to progressively learn when to rely on authority and when to undertake one's own first-hand inquiry by first-hand experience.

Having paid my respects to authority, I will say that I think the world would be better off if each person who is reasonably intelligent and has some inclination to think things out for himself, instead of accepting a pattern of belief given to him by indoctrination, tradition and convention, should try to develop his own religion; that is, if he should try to search out for himself a basis for his beliefs and con-

---

[1] This account is from memory of what happened fifty years ago. It is probable that as to at least a part of the judicial decisions referred to I had available only summarized reports of the decisions. Had the full text of the court's opinion been available in every case it is quite possible that some mention might have been found of the mathematical incongruity of the long line of decisions.

30

victions. In that effort he would, of course, endeavor to profit by the experience of others. He should have greater interest in the conclusions of those who have competently inquired than of those who have not questioned the particular traditions in which they were reared, or in which they were powerfully indoctrinated.

In a free and well matured society there might be about as many religions as there would be intelligent, inquiring people, because each person within the range of his ability and opportunity to inquire would have arrived at his own basis for thought and action. If everyone should do that it would necessarily turn out that many people would have arrived at somewhat the same pattern of belief, and people of somewhat similar belief and conviction would begin to communicate and to associate. There would begin to be fellowships based on the result of free search for truth and value, rather than on the uniformity of traditional and arbitrary authority. That, I believe, would represent an advance in the human situation.

No Revelation. Many people feel that they have had their beliefs confirmed by assurances from divine sources from without themselves. The followers of various strikingly different beliefs claim such assurance for their several specific faiths. I do not feel that I have such assurances. Convictions have come to me, sometimes through family or social tradition; sometimes through the example of sincere and purposeful, but fallible, men; sometimes from my own experience, observation and reflection; sometimes as an expression of that inner aspiration and impulse to achieve perfection which seems to be inherent in all life. I believe that these convictions are the results of human experience, insight and judgment, and of that complex resultant of many influences which goes by the name of intuition. I believe that all these sources of conviction, while helpful, are subject to error. I see my own judgment changing as experience throws more light on the questions I put to myself.

31

Man Is a Part of Nature. So far as I can see, we have no evidence that men have any especially protected place or status in the universe, or that they are immune from the working of what we call natural law; that is, from the normal processes of nature. In the course of evolution many millions of species of plants and animals have come into being, each pursuing its own destiny, but each of which has got into a "blind alley" and has become extinct, sometimes leaving fossil remains in the ancient rocks. Only a relatively few species, it seems, have successfully projected their biological inheritance into the future and have living descendants. The able and statistically-minded paleontologist, G. G. Simpson, of Columbia University and the American Museum of Natural History, refers to "thousands of millions" of species which have populated the earth.

In an article in *Evolution*[2] Simpson refers to estimates or guesses which have been made as to the number of species that have existed. The minimum estimate, which he considers far too low, is fifty million. The maximum estimate or guess is four thousand million species; a medial guess, three hundred and forty million. Of all the species that have existed, he states, "It is a conservative guess that less than ten per cent now have living descendants." At present there are estimated to be about two million living species, which have descended from a relatively few common ancestors. For instance, the insects, which make up about three quarters of all existing species of plants and animals, doubtless are descended from a single species. Shortly before the age of mammals there were "many thousands of species of mammal-like reptiles." Of all such species that existed at a given time, only two have living descendants. In short, it would seem that of the many millions of species that have emerged in the course of evolution, probably more than ninety per cent have been failures; that is, after having spent thousands or millions of

---

[2]September, 1952.

years in trying to achieve stability and survival, they have become extinct, without descendants.

I do not see that there is any assurance from above that the human race is surely protected from similar extinction. While I do not know that there is not a personal loving oversight and guidance of men outside the general frame of nature, I do not see any convincing evidence of it, and the claims of other men to such evidence do not seem convincing to me.

It seems to me that we are taking our chances with life as other species are, but with a certain difference from other species. The quality of intelligence which has developed in man, the ability to relate cause and effect, the capacity to reflect, to generalize, and then to check generalization by reflection and by further experience; these qualities, so far as I can see, do not exist in any marked degree in any other species of animal. They give man considerable control over the direction of his biological and social evolution, and give him some degree of freedom from the natural circumstances which otherwise would be his master. The long-time success or failure of the human adventure may depend on how man uses those distinctly human qualities.

I seem to observe a sort of hierarchy of nature. The inanimate world discloses certain uniformities which we call natural laws. The biological world has its own laws and manner of action which, so far as men can now see, could not be inferred from observing the inorganic world. The biological world does not escape from or nullify the natural laws of the inorganic world, but while fully subject to them it transcends them and evolves a far greater range of variety and of organization. For instance, for every inorganic compound that is known to exist, there may be a thousand organic compounds. Yet for all the vast increase of range of form of the organic world, there is no escape from the natural laws of the inorganic world of matter and energy. To understand the world of organic life it is necessary to understand the laws of matter and energy (chemistry and physics) which define the course of the material world, whether organic or inorganic.

The world of human reason and purpose transcends the biological world as the biological world transcends the world of inanimate matter and energy. But human life does not nullify the laws of the biological world. Human intelligence and purpose build upon and transcend biological life, but do not escape from its laws. Effort to understand human life without effort also to understand the physical and the biological worlds will lead to speculative fantasy, to mythology and to confusion. A large part of the concerns of religion and of ethics and morals in fact deal with the biological nature of man. To try to deal with those issues without a general knowledge of man's biological nature is bound to be erratic, confusing, and to a considerable degree ineffective. The occasional references I make to man's biological nature are not accidental or capricious, but represent my conviction that in trying to understand the human situation I must try to understand its biological elements.

IV DILEMMA AND ETHICS

ONE OF THE GREAT, but not generally recognized, facts of life is the existence of inherent dilemmas in the organic world. We have been unconsciously indoctrinated with the theological belief that all that exists or takes place is in accord with infinite understanding and with competent, adequate, divine planning. The possibility of inherent unsolved problems and of deepseated, real, unresolved dilemmas in the nature and the course of life is foreign to our thinking. Yet there seem to be real conflicts and dilemmas in essential life processes.

One of these dilemmas, I believe, is a cause of an undue sense of dependence in men. It is imperative for the continuance of human life and society that each generation shall inherit the socially accumulated cultures and skills. Each person cannot create the whole of the wisdom and culture and skill he needs to live by, but must take over much of it from the previous generations. This transmission from generation to generation cannot be left to chance. One of the chief methods used by nature to achieve this for the human species is that infancy and early childhood are very impressionable and take on the manners, attitudes and character of the human world they live in. The more dominant of these impressions tend to persist throughout life, so much a part of ourselves that we often mistake them for inborn traits, or call them second nature and rely on them as the very truth.

Where some experience of early life is nearly universal we will find a nearly universal corresponding attitude which will intrench itself in acceptance, loyalties, doctrines and ceremonials. This susceptibility to early influences is undiscriminating. It often does not distinguish between those impressions that are appropriate to the whole of life and those which

35

are suitable chiefly to the temporary conditions of infancy and early childhood.

One of the experiences of infancy and childhood is that of being immature and weak, dependent on the protection and care of greater maturity and strength, especially of parents. Few other human experiences are so universal, so pervasive, so penetrating, so unqualified. By what might be termed this accidental circumstance of fate, these experiences of personal inadequacy and of leaning on parents for support come at a time when experiences are making their deepest and most enduring imprint on personality. "What comes in with the mother's milk goes out only with the soul." This early experience of dependence tends to fix for life an attitude of dependence and of craving for support of parents or something which will take the place of parents. The dilemma is that human personality is conditioned by all its experiences, not just those that are appropriate to the whole of its life, and this feeling of weakness and inadequacy which is peculiarly appropriate to childhood lives on when it is no longer appropriate.

During childhood and adolescence a counter-instinct appears of rebellion against parental control, which often is awkward, and sometimes harmful, in its action; but it seldom erases the early impression of dependence on parents. The relative strength of the feeling of dependence and of the craving for independence varies greatly in different individuals, and is given different emphasis by different writers.

Because this feeling of inadequacy and need of support is a universal human experience just at the time when life habits are being fixed, it continues as one of the universal human traits, and finds expression in much of social and religious attitudes. It especially serves the purpose of those who wish to maintain dominance for themselves or for their systems or organizations. Acceptance of this attitude becomes a mark of virtue, and to question it has often been a crime in

36

civil life, and a sin in religion. As earthly parents disappear or prove fallible, the individual seeks new parents or their equivalent. The king and the priest take their place, while the deity is conceived as a super parent. Instead of being recognized as a defect in the cultural inheritance, this craving to lean on a parent or a substitute becomes sanctified and glorified in religion, and made the basis of loyalty in much of government.

Considering the universality and penetrating quality of this experience of dependence, we can see that the emotional weaning of men, and their emotional maturity, will not be quickly or easily achieved. Democracy assumes such maturity, but has to bear this heavy load of craving for a parent or superparent on which to be dependent. The survival of democracy in America is threatened by the desire of many persons to find some man or authority on which to lean. In the field of religion it is interesting to note how very many adherents those religions have which presume to speak with authority as would a father to a small child, and the small number of adherents of those fellowships which assume maturity and self-direction on the part of their members. Authority in religion undermines self-reliance in its followers, and this uncritical acceptance of authority affects civil life as well, and greatly weakens the democratic temper. It is difficult for a man to live half slave and half free—a slave to authority in religion, while an independent thinker in civil and political life.

Should there be a general recognition of the origin and nature of this nearly universal feeling of inadequacy and of expectation of someone or something to lean on, such recognition might lead to changes of personal outlook and of public policy which would promote emotional maturity. The attitude of dependence inherited from childhood reduces the impulse and expectation of men to master circumstance. It is

37

a heavy burden on human society, and is not the best equipment for furthering human well-being. It is a genuine dilemma. Conscious, informed purpose is necessary to overcome it.

The Conflict between Long-Time and Short-Time Biological Selection. This is a discussion, not of biology, but of religion. Yet I shall ask you to bear with me while I touch on certain biological principles, for they will help to an understanding of some fundamentals of religion.

There is another dilemma of the living world which is even more universal, more disastrous to life, and yet more compelling in relation to the needs of mature life than even the dilemma of the early indoctrination of dependence in children. Man is an animal, and his life is conditioned by biological laws. Unless we understand something of biological processes, in some important respects we shall be in the dark as to his nature, and the conditions under which he must live and plan and act. Much of religious doctrine is the result of effort to explain by metaphysics what has reasonable biological explanation.

This second dilemma I refer to is the inherent conflict between biological selection for immediate benefit, and that for the long-time good of the species. Biological evolution is very slow in human terms, and in some respects seems to be directionless. I have just referred to the fact that unnumbered species of plants and animals have started out on the road of life and have fallen by the wayside and become extinct, leaving no descendants. Why has this been true? Why was not the process of evolution with them an endless road, "onward and upward forever," always progressing from where they were to better and better adaptations to life, and to greater worth and security?

There have been a number of reasons, some of which may have no relation to the dilemma I am about to describe. Sometimes there have been changes to which the inborn na-

38

ture could not adjust. For instance, moths have instincts or tropisms which lead them to fly toward the light. Then men invent candles, and the moth flies into the flame. Its inner drive plays it false in the new situation. A very long period might be necessary to eliminate that trait in moths if it should be doing a moderate amount more harm than good to the species. When I speak of the dilemma of selection I am not referring to such difficulty. Change in outward circumstance is only one of the reasons why living species run into trouble in the effort for survival.

There is a nearly universal characteristic of biological selection, an inherent dilemma in life, which probably has been one of the chief causes for the "blind alley" course of many millions of species to extinction. I shall make a general statement of this dilemma, and then will illustrate by an example. In the course of evolution by natural selection it is a primary necessity that there be unbroken continuity of generations. For any given species, if there should be a single generation in which no member of that species had offspring, the game would be lost. The same is true as to family lines within a species. If an animal has no children it will have no grandchildren. A single break for one generation is genetically as final as a break for a thousand years. The primary requirement of any organism, or in case of social animals like honey bees, the requirement of the colony, is that there be posterity.

Now the dilemma I speak of exists because of the fact that often a course of life and action which for an individual animal will result in survival and posterity for the immediately following generation, is inherently disadvantageous to the long-time survival and welfare of the species. As the generations pass, those individuals survive and have posterity for whom *survival to the next generation* is possible. An individual may be especially well fitted to contribute to the long-time survival and welfare of the species, yet unless it is fitted

39

also to survive *to the next generation* by having posterity, long-time value will not save it. Or, conversely, it may have traits harmful to the long-time good of the species, but if these traits that are harmful in the long run help it to survive to the next generation they probably will not be eliminated. What determines the immediate survival of the line of any individual is not fitness to contribute to the long-time survival and good of the species, but fitness of the particular individual concerned to survive to the next generation. Theo. G. Dobzhansky, a foremost authority on genetics and evolution, wrote in *Genetics and the Origin of Species:*

> The process of evolution is opportunistic: natural selection favors those variants useful at a given time, regardless of their eventual value. Possessing no foresight, selection always tends to suppress mutability. But opportunism leads in the long run to retribution. . . . Genetic changes become established if they confer an advantage on their carriers at a given time and place, regardless of whether such changes might be favorable or otherwise in the long run. Any adaptive peak, however temporary, is occupied by a population, provided only that peak is accessible.

Especially among subhuman animals, living in the interest of far-off generations will not save the present or the immediately succeeding generation. The species consists only of individuals and the progeny of individuals who have succeeded in surviving to the next generation. Thus "natural selection" in some important respects seems to be short-sighted. I shall illustrate with a general class of cases, and with a particular example.

In many species sex competition at breeding time is intense. It tends to determine which of several males in a group or in a limited territory shall have posterity. In some species sex competition is so intense as to be a handicap to the species as a whole.

40

As a particular example of this general class, the American moose seems to be in that position. The bull moose each year raises great horns or antlers which have a spread of four to six feet. The chief use of these is in the breeding season, from mid-September to mid-October, to overcome other bull moose for the control of females. The antlers drop off about three months after the breeding season. For some time before that they are becoming loosened from the head somewhat as a scab comes loose from a healing wound, and that process cannot be hurried without danger, so the antlers cannot be used for fighting. New ones begin to grow in April, making the full growth of perhaps fifty pounds or more in about three months. For much of that time they are soft, pulpy and full of blood, so that damage to them may lead to serious bleeding or even to death. With its antlers in that condition the bull moose dare not use them for fighting. The calves are born in May, and when they most need protection from wolves or other natural enemies the father cannot protect them. He is hiding in the brush or up to his neck in the lake, raising new antlers just so he can fight other bull moose in the breeding season. The mother moose, who has no antlers, must protect the young.

Thus the antlers are used chiefly in deciding whether this individual or that individual is going to have offspring. The bull moose puts a large part of the energy of his life, not in overcoming natural hazards in general, but in overcoming other bull moose. If none had antlers, the species as a whole probably would be better fitted to survive; but if any single bull moose should omit having antlers and so should be available for protecting its young when protection is most needed, then it would lose out in competition with the others which do have antlers, and so it would fail to have posterity. Thus the species as a whole, in this respect at least, apparently is in a blind alley of evolution, just as numberless other species have been from various similar causes. The advantage of one

41

individual bull moose over another individual in insuring posterity for the next generation, rather than the survival and
long-time welfare of the species as a whole, has controlled
the course of evolution of the species.[1]

Doubtless the more powerful of the bull moose are vic-
torious in these contests, and so the vigor of the species may
be maintained. Also, the antlers may be defensive as well as
offensive weapons, in that they may keep the moose at some
distance from each other, thereby preventing them from cutting each other's throats with their sharp hooves. Yet on the
whole the antlers seem to be a handicap to the survival of the
species.

There are various other ways besides competitive breeding in which this conflict between immediate and long-time
interests is evident. Repeatedly the biologist comes upon such

---

[1] In the nearly endless variations which occur in the course of
animal evolution we see some devices emerging which incline
to avoid this particular dilemma of excessive sex competition.
Among honey bees the workers have unrestrained bravery,
and unhesitatingly give their lives for the protection of the
hive. But the workers do not have offspring, so cowardice
does not have individual survival value for them. The male
bees (drones) may live out of the hive only for a few hours
or a few days, long enough to fertilize the queen. After that
the queen lives isolated in her hive. The risk of battle with
the outside world is taken by the workers, who have little
concern with personal survival. Thus sex competition has
small part in the life of the honey bee, and courage and cowardice do not present an ethical dilemma. Perhaps partly because of this fact, social bees and wasps avoided this particular blind alley of evolution. Some of the same species exist
today that lived fifty million years ago, when some individuals became imbedded in pitch which turned into amber. Also,
the complex nature of the hive made evolutionary change inherently slow.

cases. It seems to be a fairly universal biological fact that what controls survival from generation to generation in the lower animals is not primarily the ability to contribute to the long-time survival and well-being of the species, but ability of individuals to survive to the next generation and to have posterity. Immediate effectiveness cannot be postponed in the interest of long-time effectiveness, which must take second place. This dilemma probably has greatly slowed the pace of evolution, and has contributed to making failures of species more frequent than successful survival. It is a chief reason why numberless species, the individual members of which were bent on securing individual survival and posterity to the next generation and have failed to serve the long-time needs of the species, have become extinct, leaving no descendants. This discrepancy between the short-time and the long-time interests of living species is one of the great dilemmas of the living world, of which man is a part. I have repeated this idea over and over to emphasize it because it represents a fundamental and highly important biological and social truth which seldom is clearly presented.

Sometimes the same quality which helps the individual to survive from generation to generation also contributes to the long-time survival of the species. That fact will be illustrated a little further on.

Religion Is in Essence a Way to Accelerate Evolution. Now, I repeat, this is not a discussion of biology, but is about religion. This seeming diversion has been to help to an understanding of human morals and ethics. For this great dilemma of the incongruity between the requirements of immediate interest or survival, and the long-time good, runs not only through the plant and lower animal worlds, but through human life as well. It is at the very heart of the problem of morals and ethics, and of practical applied religion. It is one

43

of the greatest of all issues of the social as well as of the biological world. Religion in its moral and ethical phases is largely effort to resolve this dilemma, and much of conventional theology unknowingly and stumblingly tries to interpret that dilemma and to deal with it.

To a considerable degree, morals, ethics and religion in effect are evidence of the long-time judgment of men that biological evolution is too slow and too uncertain to fulfill human possibilities, and they are efforts to improve on nature. This would be strange language to those who originated concepts and standards of morals and ethics, and who had no clear knowledge of the evolutionary process. Yet that, in essence, is just what they were trying to do. Let me illustrate.

Take the matter of honesty. If we should have a society in which everyone was honest; in which people always dealt fairly with each other; in which there was no cheating or lying or misrepresentation or stealing, what a fine and what a powerful society that would be! All the vast effort and waste motion of practicing deceit of every kind, and of guarding against and of overcoming deceit, would be saved. Mutual confidence would tend to good will. The energies saved could be used in fulfilling the purposes of life and of society. A society in which people could fully trust each other would be immeasurably stronger than one in which there was general deceit, misrepresentation, betrayal and distrust.

A dilemma arises from the fact that deceit often achieves an immediate end. It has survival value. If that were not the case, it might long ago have been eliminated from human traits. As the person said who got his biblical texts mixed, "A lie is an abomination unto the Lord, but a very present help in time of trouble." The waste of deceit persists in society because often it helps to the immediate survival of the individual, though in the long run it is a tremendous disadvantage to the human species, and to any large society.

44

Sometimes a course which leads to immediate survival also contributes to long-time strength and survival of the species or of the society involved. It is an important fact, especially in human society, that very contrary traits may have survival value at the same time. Where that condition exists, a trait which has both long-time and short-time value will tend to gain ground over a trait which has only short-time value. This is the case with honesty and dishonesty. I remember two stores on the same street in a town where I lived. One of them had been owned and operated for three generations by a family of integrity. All through the town there were people who traded at that store because it was fully trustworthy, and it had become the largest store in town. Honesty had value, not only for the long run, but for the present. Had honesty no immediate survival value, the honestly run store probably would have died.

The other store was operated by people who advertised loudly and without much regard for truth. Its prices were lower, and its goods of less dependable quality. There were enough strangers in the town at any time, and enough persons who were undiscriminating or gullible, or who themselves trusted to their shrewdness rather than to honesty, to supply many customers. That store also became one of the largest in town, though in two or three generations it failed through a mistake in policy and planning. So here were two contrary standards of action, each having survival value. Each found profit in its way of life. One contributed to improving the quality of the general life, the other for a time to its debasement.

I repeat, evolution through biological selection, through the changing of deeply imbedded biological traits, usually is very slow. A lower animal or a person may have a trait that, especially as it relates to the long-time welfare and continuity of the species, is out of date. In the natural course of events many thousands of years might pass before such a trait might be eliminated by biological selection.[2]

But in the human breed there has emerged something which seemingly does not exist in other animal species, except in rudimentary form; a way by which a very long and slow evolutionary process can be short-circuited to secure desirable results in a relatively short time. I refer to intelligence, and especially to reflective thinking.

To a considerable degree men can understand the effects of their actions; they can consider the long-range as well as the short-time results. Repeatedly they observe instances in which undisciplined biological impulses or socially traditional ways of acting are in conflict with the long-range interests of society, or in which the interest in immediate individual success or survival contravenes the long-time social good; and they see other types of action which would better serve long-time interests. Then, by intelligent purposefulness they drive toward types of thought and action which they believe will have long-time value. As to many human relationships there has come to be a general judgment of mankind that certain unrestrained impulses, and certain actions and attitudes aimed at serving immediate personal survival and increase as

---

[2]Many or most species have in their genetic inheritance large reservoirs of seldom used and half-suppressed traits which, perhaps present in only a small proportion of individuals, under changing circumstances may be so useful as to save the species from extinction. For instance, the chemical D.D.T. would kill most flies, but a few are immune to its effects, and when D.D.T. has been freely used, as in a health project in some villages in Egypt, the descendants of the few that did survive multiplied rapidly and in a few years have produced a race of flies which would not be killed by that chemical. The possession by a species of a large reservoir of recessive or largely hidden traits seems to be a major resource of many species in adjusting to changes of environment.

46

contrasted to the general social good, shall be discouraged or eliminated by outward control or by the stimulating of inward ethical motive and discipline.

To bring current action into accord with long-time social good, men set up standards of action in the form of laws, ethical or moral principles, and "good manners." They say in effect, "You have inclination to act in a way that is injurious to society. This other way is how you should act in the long-time interest of society." Thus, in the effort to deal practically with this age-old and universal dilemma of immediate interest in conflict with long-time good, we have the origin of law, ethics and morals, and of much of religious doctrine. Sometimes in order to make these practical judgments more acceptable and effective, they have been presented in the form of commands or revelations from the gods.[3]

Let us illustrate this process by the manner of dealing with the impulse to revenge. We are familiar with the saying, "Revenge is sweet to the savage soul." In many other species of animals, as well as in men, there seems to be an inborn im-

---

[3]We see the emergence of long-range ethical convictions in many stages. The ethical principle of commitment to honesty is having a slow, halting acceptance. Among the Spartans, as among some present-day primitive cultures, deceit in some cases has been held to be a religious virtue, as it is held to be a civic virtue in Communism and in the military intelligence and other spy services of our own and other governments. In the folk tales of nearly all peoples, shrewd dishonesty is looked upon as a desirable trait. The stories of "Brer Rabbit," which are African folk tales, are examples. Yet, so far as intelligent, objective ethical thinking prevails, I believe that honesty is increasingly recognized as a long-time value. If it has long-time value in the nature of things and regardless of people's present opinions in the matter, then it is inherently ethical.

47

pulse to retaliate when wronged or injured. But society as a whole finds that for the individual to take revenge on someone who he believes has harmed him is a disturbing and disrupting social habit, which does so much harm that it cannot be tolerated. Society has concluded that it must reserve to itself the redressing of wrongs. So it sets up laws that in various ways check the practice of "sweet revenge." You must not murder your neighbor because he has wronged you. You must not slander him. And then religious doctrines or teachings carry the control further—from outward restraint to inner motive. There is the counsel, "Love your enemy," forgive the wrong done you. "Ye have heard it hath been said, 'An eye for an eye and a tooth for a tooth,' but I say unto you that ye resist not evil." Thus society, through laws, manners, morals and religion, recognizes the conflicts between biological impulse or old social tradition as to retaliation on the one hand, and the long-time good of society on the other.

It may not always be true in our society that "honesty is the best policy." However, if one has lived honestly, even at great disadvantage to himself, he will be helping to create a social atmosphere in which honesty *is in fact the best policy*. For one to take that course is truly creative living. Probably the present strong foothold honesty has in society was won by many generations of just such creative effort. Laws, manners, morals and religion are largely efforts to resolve that fundamental dilemma of life, the incompatibility of short-time or personal interest with long-time social good. Religion and morals are to some extent efforts to create social atmosphere in which the long-time good will also be advantageous in the short run, as for instance in creating a society in which honesty *is* the best policy. Ethical standards cut across the long, slow process of natural selection and aim directly at the ends which can be seen by intelligence. Dobzhansky wrote: "Cultural evolution is a process which is vastly more rapid and more efficient than biological evolution."

48

In some cases recognition of the need to act in accord with long-time social good, rather than for immediate personal survival, has become deeply imbedded in society. Patriotism is such a case. The soldier, if he is active in fighting, is apt to be killed and so cut off from personal posterity. He might run away and thereby increase his prospect of having personal descendants. But his impulse to act in accord with the good of his tribe or country controls over his impulse to act in accord with his own individual welfare by running away. That determination to act according to the general, long-time good of one's group—it may be a very circumscribed and provincial group—rather than for one's own personal survival or interest, that is ethical or moral action. Patriotism doubtless originated in small, closely knit tribal groups where it was obvious that the entire tribe was "in the same boat," and where "unless they should hang together they would hang separately." In such circumstances the gap between short-time personal welfare and long-time social welfare was not great, and little imagination was necessary to bridge it. Morals doubtless began in such simple and obvious relationships, and have gradually been extended to wider and more distant relationships. Ethics and morals exist in large part for the future.

Long before the days of modern biology and of the theory of evolution men endeavored to explain this ever-apparent dilemma and conflict between biological drives or unsuitable social conditioning on the one hand, and the general welfare on the other; between the pressure for immediate individual survival and the often conflicting needs of long-time social welfare. From that effort at explanation arose the doctrines of temptation, sin, and total depravity. The impulse to act in accord with undisciplined biological drive or undesirable social tradition, or the tendency to assure immediate individual survival and posterity regardless of the long-time social good—that was "temptation." The yielding to such impulse was "sin." The persistent and nearly universal impulse to act in accord with some socially harmful biological drives, or to insure personal survival and posterity regardless of long-time social good, was "original sin" or "total depravity."

Social vs. Genetic Value. The appraisals and interpretations of ethical and spiritual leaders in prescientific times had large elements of truth and wisdom which we do well to recognize and respect, even when they are associated with fabulous philosophical or theological explanations. In a biological sense men to a large degree are brothers. The genetic inheritance they have in common is far greater than that which is peculiar to a person, a family or a tribe. (This is not to minimize individual and family differences in genetic inheritance, or the importance of eugenic considerations.) As to a majority of individuals it may make but limited genetic difference to the species which ones survive and have posterity, and which do not. (That statement requires clarification and qualification for which I will not take time.) As to the greater part of most populations there probably is more difference between good and bad, between mediocrity and excellence, in the social than in the inborn inheritance. As to the greater part of any large population it probably is at least as important which of the existing social and ethical patterns survive as what particular genetic strains continue, though that might not be true in all cases. The vision and character of the great world leaders have been more important to the future than their sons and daughters, though here too, the relative value of individuals is a matter of cases and of degrees. For Jesus to have compromised his convictions in order to survive and have children probably would have been an over-all loss to humanity. As Arnold Winkelreid of Swiss legend, by gathering the enemy spears to his breast breached the enemy line and made way for victory at the cost of his life, so the ethical pioneer, in living for the long-time interests of men at the

50

cost of his interests or of his life, and perhaps at the cost of having personal posterity, may help to create a social atmosphere favorable to the long-time good.

Ethics and morals provide a way for accelerating evolution. That is their chief value. A trait survives best in an atmosphere of its kind. Honesty survives best in a society where people are honest. When a man by being honest in a partly dishonest society helps to make an honest environment he is creating an atmosphere favorable to the survival of honesty. He is actually and directly accelerating social evolution.

A person naturally strives for his own survival. "He" is made up of traits. If an environment favors those traits it favors his survival. In an effort to survive he is loyal to his own traits whether they are good or bad from a long-time social standpoint. I used to wonder why it was that a college student with antisocial traits was not satisfied to express them himself, but actually propagandized to spread those traits in the student body. He was in effect trying to create an environment which would be favorable to his own survival. The prohibition and the antiprohibition campaigns were of that nature.

Beyond "Adaptation." With natural selection in the animal world, adaptation to the immediate environment is the ruling tendency. With men it need not be so. The religious man, the ethical man, the spiritual man, undertakes to adjust, not to the world that is, but to the world that might be and ought to be; to the ideal world, using the term "ideal" to mean the best that might be. In doing so he participates in creating the atmosphere of that kind of world, in which men with traits in harmony with the long-time general good would be at home, and would survive.

With the process of adapting to the present world, a vast duration of time might be required for genetic and social

51

traits which serve the long-time general good to become dominant in society. With conscious aiming directly at the traits of a good society through ethical living, the time required for such a change might be very greatly reduced. What might require tens of thousands of years by the first process might be reduced to a few centuries or even to a few generations by the second. Through recorded human history these two processes have been active together, often in sharp conflict, and progress toward a good society has been slow.

One reason why ethical living has made no more progress is that ethical standards often have been arrived at by emotional reaction from unethical extremes, and have really defeated their ends. For instance, it is recorded that at a time when Egypt was solidly Christian the dogmatic reaction from sensual living was so strong that half the Egyptian population was in monasteries and nunneries; that is, the ethically sensitive part of the population was being methodically exterminated. The same process operated among the Bogomils, who at one time gave promise of transmitting to Europe a fine general type of culture. In America the same interpretation of right living eliminated the Shakers. These are extreme cases to illustrate the principle that ethical standards arrived at by uninformed intuition—often called revelation—may be so destructive that the natural selection of the animal world may be better. This may be true of our own ethical codes as well as of those of other times and other cultures. If life is to be ruled by ethical direction, rather than by raw natural selection, then it is imperative that ethical standards be appraised and disciplined by free critical inquiry as well as by the general sense of fitness of men.

Where life is lived by tradition, dogma, custom or instinct, what survives is a total life pattern, which is very complex and a mixture of good and bad elements. The whole pattern tends to be accepted, supported and defended as one, even though its elements are essentially incongruous. For

52

instance, in practically every Christian country which is firmly in the control of an orthodox religious hierarchy, there is extreme exploitation of the poor by the rich. Incongruous elements have been associated in the one pattern for more than a thousand years.

Where critical ethical inquiry prevails the total culture can be examined element by element, the desirable components can be strengthened and the undesirable ones reduced or eliminated, and a new social species may emerge by conscious selection. Thus social evolution can be accelerated, not only by conscious favoring of one pattern over another, but also by selection of traits within a social pattern.

Ethical excellence should be measured, not chiefly by the degree of conformity to any prevailing conventional pattern, but by presence of sustained, intelligent effort to achieve a valid ethical pattern and to actually live by it. There is a great contrast between responsible and concerned self-direction on the one hand, and on the other hand undisciplined drifting in servitude to animal impulse or to undiscriminating custom.

53

V THE NATURE OF VALUE

WHAT IS VALUE? A conventional definition of value is, "The quality or fact of being worth while, excellent, useful, or desirable; worth in a thing, whether real or imputed." For our purposes such a definition can be made more definite. Insofar as I can discern, value is always associated with life; where there is no life or prospect of life, there can be no value. *Value is experience which those who have it feel that it is better to have than not to have, and anything which contributes to such experience.*[1] We value money, land, goods, influence, because we believe they will help us to have experience which it is better to have than not to have. In love, friendship, patriotism and other group affection one becomes part of a larger self, and in relation to that larger self the same definition holds. *Possible* experience

---

[1]The technical philosopher will object to the latter part of this definition. He will say that "anything which contributes to a desirable experience" is not a value, but an effective instrument for achieving value. Obviously this book is written, not primarily for the technical philosopher or psychologist, but for the general reader. Here, and throughout the book, there is effort to avoid technical terms or technical explanations which, while appropriate in writing for professional philosophers or psychologists or biologists, would cumber the general reader without adding appreciably to his understanding of the subject. For instance, in contrast to the everyday use of the term "value" as something desirable, to the professional philosopher it means anything which commands interest, either favorable or unfavorable. According to such a definition, an experience which it is better not to have than to have would be a negative value. I have used the term "value" in the common, everyday sense of relating only to what is desirable.

54

which those who would have it would feel it to be better to
have than not to have, we may call *potential* value. According to this definition, experience which it is better not to have
than to have is the opposite of value. We learn about values
by experiencing them at first hand, and otherwise by the
same processes as those by which we acquire other knowledge.

There are many kinds, degrees and qualities of values as
to unalloyedness, intensity, duration, harmony or disharmony
with other values or the values of others or the values of the
future, etc. Of experiences which are good in themselves,
some are casual, superficial, trivial; some are enduring and
deep. Intelligent purpose is necessary to distinguish, both in
thought and in action, between values that are transient and
those that are enduring, between those that are superficial
and trivial and those that are deep, those that conflict with
or eliminate other values, and those which harmonize with
the whole of a good pattern of life.

Sometimes the values we experience have complex relationships. Take opium, for instance. After a dose of opium
the heavens open and the addict has a period of ecstasy, of
near perfect happiness. Such happiness is a real value. But
then it is paid for by a terrible experience of depression, illness, and discomfort. The addict is in hell, after having been
in heaven. Not only is there that short alteration of experience but, what is far more serious, there is a progressive
destruction of physical and mental health which leaves the
opium user a miserable wreck, with will and self-control
destroyed. The evanescent experience of happiness was a
value, but not worth the price. We have many values in life
that are not worth the price. "Revenge is sweet," but the
sweetness is outweighed by the total cost. The eating of good
food is an experience desirable in itself. It is a value both as
an immediate experience and as a contribution to fitness for
living. Yet if that particular value is experienced without relation to other values we may have gluttony, which will injure

55

health and so interfere with other and greater values than the pleasure of unrestrained eating. The art of living, and ethics, morals and religion, originate largely in efforts to guide men in distinguishing and in choosing between the greater and the less, between the better and the worse, of experiences which men feel to be good. The function of ethics, morals and religion is to encourage ways of life which will lead to the selection of the more enduring and significant values.

To this definition of value, as experience which one feels it is better to have than not to have, some people will cry "hedonism." I have tried to understand what the great religions of the world promise; that is, what they present as values; what would they keep men away from, and what would they draw men to. Almost universally the great religions claim to point the way to increase of a sense of well-being, to an increase of felicity or happiness. Consider the "Sermon on the Mount." It promises "blessedness." "Blessed are the meek," "Blessed are the merciful, the peacemakers." "Great is your reward in heaven." We think of the Christian ethic as being as high as any. Yet the Christian ethic presents this as the proper human aim. "Blessed are ye," that is, if you act in a certain way you will have a desirable sense of having experience which it is better to have than not to have.

Job, in the depth of his affliction, said of his God: "Though he slay me, yet will I trust him." This has been interpreted as recognition of value beyond desirable experience. Yet a careful reading will make it clear that what Job most valued was a deep assurance that God would remove his undesirable experience and provide desirable experience.

When I think of what it is we desire when we search for a way of life, when I observe what great religions have promised us, I do not find anything more than that the amount, quality, intensity, and duration of desirable experience shall increase, and that their opposite shall decrease. "Sorrow and sighing shall flee away." This over-all hope and expectation are expressed in many ways. Christian hymnology informs us that when we go to heaven we shall wear golden crowns, shall play on golden harps and walk the golden streets. We shall have ecstatic experiences without satiety. Aristotle pictured a more refined joy of free contemplation, or of the fullfilment of one's essential function, but still nothing beyond desirable experience.

The generalizing and idealizing impulse which is characteristic of all life operates in the field of values. We crave values that will justify our sustained loyalty and interest. Man takes his imperfect values and idealizes them by trying to see them as they would be fully developed and without blemish. He is not free to complete them in any way his fancy leads. To be true to himself and his values he must idealize them and complete them according to their nature. Max Planck, the originator of the quantum theory, wrote in discussing "Hypothesis": "It must be free from everything in the nature of logical incoherence. Otherwise the researcher has an entirely free hand."

We may illustrate from the inorganic world. Quartz crystals have certain characteristics in common. Between two similar (homologous) sides of any such crystal the angle is always the same; but the similar sides are not always the same length or width in different quartz crystals. There are endless shapes and sizes, yet every one follows the same laws of crystallization.

Nearly all quartz crystals are imperfect. The need for a base on which to rest or by which to be supported usually means that one side or end blends with the surounding rock, and so the crystal is marred. From our knowledge of the nature of quartz crystals and from our capacity to generalize we may picture to ourselves what a perfect one would be like. As scientists we are not free to complete that crystal in our minds in any way we will; as for instance, to visualize it as completed after the nature of a garnet or a diamond crystal. Re-

57

sponsible idealizing or generalizing will lead us to complete the design in our minds according to the nature of quartz crystals.

Is such an idealization a fancy or a myth, or has it certain elements of faith? If no complete, unmarred quartz crystal ever had been found, the ideal pattern of a complete, unmarred crystal might have been termed a fantasy, a myth, a hypothesis, a fiction, a generalization, an archetype, or by some other similar name, depending on the philosophical pattern of the person speaking. A seemingly reasonable dogma might be developed to the effect that since gravity is universal, and since a quartz crystal must of necessity have a support during its formation, therefore it is inevitable that every one should be marred on one side or end, and that a complete, unmarred specimen is a practical impossibility. In tramping over the mountains of southwest Newfoundland, exploring small cavities in a rock face I came across some complete quartz crystals, whole and unmarred. Similar perfect specimens have been found in Herkimer County, New York. Evidently some kind of mineral was present during the formation of the crystal which was dense enough to support it while it was growing, but of a character which did not interfere with its perfect formation. The actual finding of such perfection gives a sense of assurance of its possibility which no theorizing would provide, at least for the average man.

Men take fragments and rudiments of values which they see functioning around them in society, and by disciplined, creative imagination they achieve great and fine patterns of value, which may become their most highly treasured possessions. The "Sermon on the Mount" of Christian literature, and similar expressions of other faiths, are examples. We may call these ideals, dreams, revelations or hypotheses. If they truly picture the unmarred realization of innate potentiality it may not be far amiss to call them truths.

Such ideal values seldom take form by reason alone. They come by experience, teaching, aspiration, intuition, and by the seemingly sudden opening of the mind to new possibilities which often goes by the name of inspiration. They come to persons who, by favorable constitution and by consistent nurture of the spirit, are prepared for them. People attach their faith and hope to these patterns of value, even when they have been created from fragments of reality. Their faith and hope are greatly strengthened if they see actual embodiments of these values in people's lives. For that reason, examples of good living are among the most powerful influences among men.

Among liberal, semi-orthodox Christians it is common to look upon Jesus as the perfect exemplification of the possibilities of humanity. This desire for a perfect example led to the formation of a dogma that such was the case, though the historical evidence is far too meager to fully establish the fact.

Science Is Concerned with Values. It frequently has been stated, both by scientists and by men of "religion," that science is not concerned with values, but only with facts and with conclusions drawn from them. Men of "religion," claiming to be especially ordained for the moral ordering of life, are inclined to order scientists out of their sacred domain. On the other hand, partly from a desire to be left alone, unmolested in their own field, scientists often are willing to make truce with the theologians on that point. I believe that is a false position. Dealing with values is, I think, the main issue of life, and a valid issue of science. When scientists agree to leave values to men of religion they are, it seems to me, surrendering their right to a share in the kingdom, and are settling for the administration of a province.

Yet some ranking scientists have taken that view. Max Planck wrote in his autobiography, "All the problems of ethics are outside the field of natural science." Again he wrote, "If we ascribe to God, in addition to His omnipotence and omniscience, also the attributes of goodness and love, recourse to Him produces an increased feeling of safety and

59

happiness in the human being thirsting for solace. Against this conception not even the slightest objection can be raised from the point of view of natural science, for as we pointed out before, questions of ethics are entirely outside its realm." In trying to understand the meaning of this great scientist I may be helped by his own expression of his idea of social responsibility. He wrote: "A winged angel has been regarded from time immemorial as the most beautiful symbol for a servant and messenger of God. But there can be found among persons trained in anatomy, some whose scientifically conditioned imagination does not permit them, despite their best intentions, to see any beauty in such a physiological impossibility. Nevertheless this circumstance need not have the slightest adverse effect on their religious convictions. They ought, however, to be on their guard not to impair or destroy the pious attitude of those who still find solace and edification in the sight of a winged angel." One wonders whether it was not a similar sense of solicitude which led him to write: "No matter where or how far we look, nowhere do we find a contradiction between religion and natural science." Julian Huxley wrote: "If science will remember that it, as science, can lay no claim to set up values, it will allow due weight to the religious spirit."

Science as a game for its own sake, like chess, may be a harmless diversion with incidental benefits. Beyond that, science as a career, especially when it accepts support, either from public or private donated funds, or from inherited wealth must, I believe, be concerned with values. Science is an attitude of caring, and scientists should care. Without commitment to values such as loyalty to truth and desire for findings of significance, there could be no science. The very concern which science has for truth is a value and drives the scientist to seek the truth without compromise, even at great disadvantage to himself. Max Planck as a physicist was deeply concerned with values, and was sensitive to relative significance.

60

The Nature of Value

Science should be one of our major resources for the appraisal and definition of values—even for their discovery. Yet how many scientists kneel before the present-day inquisition of public opinion, like the great Galileo, and meekly confess that the proper domain of science is the observing and recording of natural phenomena, and their interpretation, and that science has no concern with values, nor any effective means for dealing with them!

Values, I hold, are not metaphysical abstractions or revealed absolutes; they are experiences which those who have them feel that it is better to have than not to have, and whatever contributes to such experience. They are proper subjects for inquiry, appraisal and comparison by science.

A case will illustrate the way in which science can contribute to the definition of values. In the field of race relations there has been a seeming conflict between two authentic values. On the one hand has been the importance of keeping races strong, uncontaminated, and fit instruments for the fulfillment of human destiny. Many sincere people have believed that among the larger races of men there are some that are superior and some that are inferior, and that the mixing of these would result in endangering the welfare of humanity. Other people have held that all men are brothers, that ethnic differences are minor as compared with likenesses, and that it is evil to bring upon the people of any race the humiliation of segregation and the lessening of social and economic opportunity. Science can give attention to this issue, and out of its greater loyalty to the truth and to the total good it can objectively and impartially explore the facts. In this field there are pressures and emotions which make it difficult but not impossible for the scientist to be scientific. The general trend of present-day judgment of scientists is that the supposed great differences of over-all quality of civilizations do not exist, and that segregation is not a value. In my opinion that inquiry has been somewhat emotionally (unscientifically) loaded on both sides, and final conclusions are not yet all in;

but a scientific process is under way which deals with values, and which already is throwing significant light on the existence and the relative importance of certain values.

Perhaps another illustration, though a seemingly trivial one, is justified. Most people like the experience of eating various sweetened foods. That experience is a value, though a minor one. Now scientists find by sound scientific methods that an excess of sweets may be the cause of grave physical disorders; that is, the value experience of eating sugar in certain quantity may impair far greater values. Science can deal with values and can throw light on their relative importance. Claude Bowman remarked, "A society giving the widest possible freedom to research would be led ultimately to an examination of every sanctioned value."

The scientific spirit is profoundly ethical. Its just requirement is that every interest it deals with must be measured by the truth. The operation of the scientific spirit may leave the priest without his rationalized justification for age-long, deeply intrenched prestige, and his unverified claim to be one of the elect of the Supreme Being. It leaves the economic exploiter without justification for his claim to the unearned product of other men's toil. It leaves the social revolutionist without adequate basis for his dogma that the weaknesses of men are chiefly due to economic exploitation, and may lead him to realize that he must be concerned with refining and disciplining his own life and purposes. These results may follow, not any confusing of science with propaganda, but the most objective examination of the data, and the most impartial conclusions from it.

At bottom, the extension of the scientific spirit is an ethical issue—one might almost say a religious issue. It is resisted chiefly because its acceptance would tend to the disclosure of the falseness of claims of special interests. Wherever we look, whether at dogmatic religion, or at economic privilege, or at political oppression, we find that their perpetuation depends largely on avoidance of free, sincere, competent scientific inquiry. One might even say with a considerable degree of truth that the course of science itself would be more rapid but for the tendency of fallible scientists to hold to their own vested interests. Max Planck, in his autobiography, discussing opposition among scientists to his discoveries, wrote, "This experience gave me also an opportunity to learn a fact—a remarkable one in my opinion: A new scientific truth does not triumph by convincing its opponents and making them see the light, but rather because its opponents eventually die, and a new generation grows up that is familiar with it." Scientists are human, and like the rest of us must make constant effort to achieve and to maintain the scientific attitude.

The scientist must measure values, not only in his scientific field, but in his life. Just as in his thinking and in reporting on his research it is primary with him that he shall not dissemble, but shall report truthfully, so in his life, if it is to be consistent with his science, he must appraise values without prejudice, and must live by his appraisal. Few factors tend more to cloud judgment than habits of living that are inconsistent with the conclusions of critical, objective inquiry.

VI CHOOSING ONE'S SPIRITUAL PARENTS

ONE OF THE GREAT FACTS OF LIFE is that to a large degree one can determine his own world of values, what he will care for and seek and work for, where his interests and satisfactions will be. One's sense of values and one's active interests can be trained, educated—largely re-created.

It is common for a person to believe that he has his particular pattern of interests because he is inherently that kind of person, and that is the end of the matter. His statement, "That does not interest me," seems to him to tell, not only what is the case, but what in the nature of things *must* be.

Only to a limited degree is that true. Obviously, the values one holds in early life are determined by his inborn traits and his early conditioning. The fact that one had no control as to who his physical parents are, or what his early environment may be, does not irretrievably set the general pattern of his fate. As one approaches adolescence and maturity he becomes more and more able to determine his mental and spiritual environment. To some extent he can select his own associations. He can exercise a degree of choice as to what he shall see and listen to by radio or television, and especially as to what he shall read.

If a purposeful man, who has developed the habit and skill of dealing effectively with circumstances, once gets the general idea that he can determine his own cultural parentage, and that he wants his system of values to be as universal, as enduring and as excellent as possible, that realization may initiate in him a revolutionary process of cultural rebirth. He can, by his reading and in various other ways, introduce himself to the greatest of the spiritual and intellectual traditions of mankind. He can choose the great spirits of the world as his cultural and spiritual parents. The proportion of men who take such a course is small, but so is the proportion of men who have sustained, long-range purpose for their lives.

One does not accomplish that by any single act of decision. Learning the language and the spirit of great men will demand more time and effort than did learning the language of one's physical parents. One must begin with ideas and language and actions that are within his reach and within his interests, and step by step grow into the language, ideas and interests of great literature, and of the men who wrote or inspired great literature. One need not take his present interests as final. That a man can educate and recreate his interests is one of the most encouraging facts about being human.

Reading or other communication is only one step in acquiring great men for one's cultural parents. Reading and saying the words, and even thinking the thoughts, of greatness will be largely sterile unless at the same time one is actually learning to live the life. Just as learning the language and spirit of great men is a gradual process, so action toward remaking one's interests may begin with relatively simple undertakings, and increase as spiritual muscle and skill are developed. One sometimes meets persons who are very well read, sometimes in the world's greatest literature, but who are essentially ineffective or who have mediocre motives, because they have not steadily practiced at living the life. That is particularly true as to persons who have read literature which concerns the ordering of life, but it is also true elsewhere. For instance, one can better get the significance of science if he not only reads but thoughtfully observes, and where possible does research. The habit of observation and original research, within the limits of one's ability and circumstances, should be as general as the habit of reading. It is within the reach of every normally intelligent person.

In short, even if one is born into a mediocre environment and is endowed with only average intelligence, if he once gets the idea and the spirit of determining his own cultural and spiritual parentage and of achieving a great pattern of values, he can surmount mediocrity. He can insure that enduring, inclusive and long-range values shall become his livest and keenest interests, and can learn to live in conformity with them. Such a discovery leads to a life of real adventure, for in the world that is it is not easy to successfully pattern one's life by greatness. The essence of adventure is the purposeful surmounting of difficulty, while facing uncertainty.

One will discover that great living has no necessary relation to conspicuous living. George Herbert wrote very truly,

> Who sweeps a room as by thy laws
> Makes that and the action fine.

That is not just poetry; it is fact. The governor of the state arriving at his position by political deals and surrender of his convictions; the corporation head, achieving his position by ruthless ambition; the author of a "best seller," who has learned how to pander successfully to mediocre public taste —none of these may have as great long-time imprint on history as the home keeper who "sweeps a room as by thy laws," and whose relations with family, neighbors and other associates are those of integrity, good will, friendliness, understanding and helpfulness. She is contributing to a texture of life by which humanity may be able to survive its stresses. Every person has such opportunity in the day's work.

If there is lacking the initial spark of aspiration and desire to remake one's personality in accord with a larger and better design, how is that spark lighted? It is chiefly by passing the fire from man to man through intimate human association. Prometheus may bring his spiritual fire only occasionally, but ordinary men can keep it burning, and by example can pass it on to others. Of the unknown proportion of men who seem totally inert to spiritual fire, I believe that the larger part have been made that way by social conditioning, rather than by genetic constitution.

66

VII THE SPIRITUAL BODY

SOMEWHAT as an individual person inherits or acquires a complex of characteristics which together constitute his personality, so any human society, large or small, which continues for a considerable time, comes to have a body of common feelings, attitudes, loyalties and standards that in their total are the personality of that society. These characteristics taken all together we may call its spiritual body. While this spiritual body is intangible, it is one of the most real and potent factors of human existence.

The essence of life that is characteristically human is in its "spiritual bodies," sometimes primitive and relatively simple, sometimes sophisticated and complex. In the total they make up human culture, and it is chiefly that culture which makes man superior to any of the other mammals. Man's very biological continuity has come to depend on them. If in some way the whole of the "spiritual bodies" of all human societies should be eliminated, what would be left would be only a very deteriorated kind of animal, unable to sustain itself. Next to sheer biological functioning, the spiritual bodies of human societies are the most necessary element and the greatest resource of the race. To ignore them, as often they are ignored, is unintelligent and perilous.

Different societies have very different spiritual bodies, some more favorable than others to the fulfillment of human possibilities. These several spiritual bodies seldom are entirely in harmony, and human life is a constant effort to harmonize and unify them. Some of them concern only trivial and casual matters. A stamp collectors' club may engender much zeal in its members, but to no important purpose. On the other hand, the spiritual body of a man's religious society may give the dominant form, pattern, meaning and incentive to his life. To destroy a man's participation in such a spiritual body may largely disrupt his life.

A person may at one time live in several societies, each with its own spiritual body, and these may interpenetrate and interact, influencing each other. A man may be an active member of a church which has a distinctive pattern of aspirations, loyalties, convictions, and habits of sharing experiences—its own spiritual body. At the same time he may be a member of the banking fraternity or of a labor union, with its characteristic pattern of attitudes, loyalties and convictions, which constitutes its spiritual body. As an active member of his community he may share the community spirit or spiritual body. He may belong to a "fine old family" with the pride and dignity which go with an honored family name. Sharing the spirit of the family, he would shrink from any action which would cloud its reputation.

All such societies influence each other. None of them is— or ought to be—free from such interaction. The church affects business and the home; the home affects church and business; business affects church and home; and so with a multitude of associations. The life philosophy and practice of a person or of a society should make it sensitive and receptive to influences which would enhance its quality, and should make it immune from any that would cause it to deteriorate.

A free people will have many free associations. Their variety will make possible a range and a richness of culture which would be impossible to any "planned" regime. In a totalitarian body, whether economic, political or religious, there is an effort to have the one totalitarian "spiritual body" dominate or displace all others. All loyalty must be to the one totalitarian society. Even family loyalty must give way, and children are taught to spy upon their parents. This was true of the totalitarian "Holy Inquisition" as well as in Communist society today. A regime which is totalitarian in spirit claims to be unique and of a different order from any other.

68

It constantly inclines to displace and to exclude any that differs from it. When it is a minority it claims or pleads for tolerance or for civil rights; when it has dominant power it strives to suppress or exclude any nonconforming element. A free society needs to be constantly on its guard against those elements which are totalitarian in spirit, and which strive gradually to take exclusive possession.

There is another ancient type of totalitarian society which exists in small units. Primitive village societies, where everyone has direct personal relations with everyone else and the whole dimensions of life are small, and where there are few associations beyond village limits, tend naturally to be totalitarian and monolithic. In them all life tends to have a single, interwoven pattern, sometimes the result of many centuries of intimate association. The "spiritual body" of such a small unit often is penetrating, inclusive and powerful, and largely controls the pattern of living. When such a primitive "spiritual body" is broken, as by the intrusion of modern civilization, often the result is disastrous. For instance, when Hawaii came into contact with the "civilized" world and became Christianized, the disruption of old ways and of life was very great, and the native population withered to perhaps a tenth of what it had been. Part of these effects were biological—lack of immunity to European diseases—but in considerable degree they were the effects of breaking the spiritual pattern. Various little primitive societies have disintegrated, died out, and the population has become extinct, chiefly from the breaking of that spiritual pattern.

The "spiritual body" of a native, "pagan" village community of West Africa is an example of those that are very strong and give form and direction to the whole life. Community moral standards are more fully observed than in most civilized communities. When individual native members are Europeanized and converted to Christianity, the indigenous "spiritual body" is thus disrupted. Very commonly the personalities of such men and women disintegrate, and the moral standards of the indigenous community break down. Until recently the missionaries, in their zeal to save men's souls from hell, and in their nearly complete ignorance of anthropology and sociology, were not aware of the values they were destroying, or that they were disrupting a spiritual body.

The Muslims often took a different course. They preserved the spiritual body of the indigenous community, but infused it with the doctrines and ethical standards of Islam, until the community, while maintaining its spiritual body, adopted Islam as its religion. Today some Christian missionaries are belatedly waking up to the realities of the situation, and are adopting a similar course.

In India until recently Christian missionaries have ignored the spiritual bodies of the indigenous villages and other societies, and have tended to disrupt them in their efforts to "save souls," and with not dissimilar results. Gandhi commented, as have others, on the fact that conversion to Christianity commonly led to a deterioration of personality, especially in the second generation of Christians which had not grown up in the spiritual body of the old indigenous society.

The Influence of the Christian Church in America. What I have written so far probably has quite completely alienated the churchman. Many of those who have repudiated the church as simply an organization of superstition and spiritual exploitation will strongly approve. While they speak truly of the crude mythology of the church, dressed though it be in the finespun robe of theology, of its refusal to honestly inquire, and of its habit of diverting men's interest and attention to its mythology and to speculative metaphysical fantasies, such disabilities are only a part of Christian culture. During more than half a century I have kept considerable contact with a great variety of Christian fellowships, ranging through Roman Catholic, Mormon, Christian Science, the

70

Greek Orthodox, "Fundamentalist," liberal Protestant, and the more traditional Protestant fellowships, such as the Episcopalian, Lutheran and Mennonite. These several bodies vary greatly in their desirable and undesirable characteristics. The Roman Catholics have to a considerable extent repudiated racial discrimination, the Baptists have vigorously upheld the separation of church and state, the Unitarians have championed free inquiry, the Mormons have emphasized the social responsibility of the members for each other, and the Methodists, Congregationalists and Friends have done pioneering work on social issues.

Such special services, however, are not the measure of the value of these religious fellowships. It is the "spiritual bodies" of these religious societies which are of greatest desirable significance. By and large, though by no means always, the churches of America have had standards of personal decency, of honesty in practical human relations, of helpfulness in time of trouble, and of mutual respect, affection and regard for their fellow members. One element of the spiritual body of many of the various religious associations is an emotional quality of aspiration (using the world "emotional" in its psychological, rather than in its popular meaning), of putting right living and a spirit of brotherhood above economic or other personal considerations. It includes the habit of constantly measuring oneself by one's ideal pattern and constantly striving to be like that pattern. This is a continuing spiritual tradition which lives from generation to generation, which keeps alive the emotional fineness that has come to it, and which is kept alive by the infection of one spirit by another, as one fire lights another.

Those who live in and share such a spiritual body commonly are favorably modified by it. Just as a pile of sticks of wood will keep burning if they are so close together that the heat from each one radiates to the others and keeps them on fire, whereas if the sticks were scattered, each by itself would

71

lose its fire; so a close fellowship of like-minded and like-spirited people tends to keep aflame the fire of aspiration, brotherhood and commitment to the best the members know. Though they may be greatly in the minority, there are many persons thus motivated. They are the spiritual life of their religious societies, and help give character to the larger society.

This spiritual body of a religious fellowship is largely emotional, rather than intellectual, but that is true of all effective living. A man's life is like an ocean vessel traveling under power. The direction in which the vessel will travel is determined by the navigator, using the steering wheel and the rudder of the vessel. The actual motion of the vessel toward its goal is determined by the power plant and its fuel. Without a power plant the vessel would only drift; with a power plant but without a rudder it would only go in circles, or would zigzag with changing wind and currents.

In a man's life, reason and emotion are equally essential. Reason gives emotion its ends and aims. Emotion moves men to the fulfillment of whatever aims they have. My difference with those in Christian countries who wholly repudiate the Christian fellowship is that while they would try to have good rudders they often are content with inadequate power plants, and have not the spiritual fuel to make them go. They desire to be intellectually right, but frequently lack that commitment of spirit and actuality of aspiration which would lead them to discipline their own lives, and to give everything they have to make their lives conform to the best they know. In them the continuity of the spiritual tradition has been interrupted. They have lost an emotional inheritance, and probably will not regain it except by infection or contagion from a living spiritual body. This is by no means uniformly true, but discontinuity of the spiritual tradition commonly is a serious loss.

My quarrel with Christian organization and theology is that their rudders are twisted, and the steering wheels are in

72

the hands of men who chart their courses by mythologies and metaphysical fantasies, rather than by the results of the process of sincere, open inquiry. Great age does not make a myth true nor a primitive metaphysics less fantastic. Most Christian fellowships would close the minds of their followers and associates to such free inquiry. Of the sermons I listen to in all parts of America, in person and over the radio, a large part of the time is given to primitive mythology and to incongruous, speculative metaphysics, commonly called doctrines or beliefs, and thus the minds of the audience are diverted from the vital spiritual tradition.

I am reminded much of the so-called paganism of Africa and other regions where fine qualities of mutual regard and responsibility and well sustained moral standards—the spiritual bodies of the societies in question—are distorted and mutilated by witchcraft, superstition and voodooism. Incidentally, much of this pagan superstition and voodooism seems to be the primitive parent of some modern religious practice. For instance, in West Africa the over-all deity is spiritual and unseen, but the subordinate deities, in modern parlance called saints, have their shrines where miracles are performed, where, as at Christian shrines, many crutches are left behind after the miracles, but never a glass eye or a wooden leg. With a few changes of names, some modern orthodox practices and these primitive pagan practices would seem strikingly alike.

The Christian ethics, as expressed in the first three gospels, seem to me to be somewhat superior to any other of the ancient systems. Our country and the world could profit much by more intimate acquaintance with these standards. Is it not a great tragedy that many of the members of most American religious fellowships have their attention and interest so centered on inherited ancient mythology and superstititon and metaphysical speculations that the emphasis on fine ethical quality is largely lost? But for that loss, the spirit of this ethic might be a far more powerful regenerating influ-

73

ence. One is tempted to provide specific instances illustrating this unfortunate condition, but I shall not do so.

The burden of these comments is that one of the greatest of all human resources, though often adulterated with grave disadvantages, is the accumulation of the "spiritual bodies" of our various voluntary associations, and that among these, Christian fellowships are important. Whoever leaves out of account these spiritual bodies is omitting one of the priceless values of humanity. For that reason, in spite of my complete departure from Christian theology, I have been loath to give up association with the spiritual bodies of Christianity.

In varying degrees most religions have similarly precious spiritual bodies. Although my associations have been chiefly with people of the Christian tradition, if I should list the half-dozen finest characters I have known, at least two spiritual bodies other than those of the Hebrew-Christian tradition would be the source of quality of persons on that very short list.

My long-time judgment is that in my search for purpose, while I should vigorously hold to freedom of inquiry and should have no arbitrary or credulous loyalty to traditional or authoritarian beliefs, either as to metaphysical theory or as to ethical standards, yet it is important that I cultivate my emotional as well as my intellectual life. I believe that the best of emotional life—of the spiritual body—is a gradually accumulated inheritance of aspiration, fellowship, self-discipline, and understanding and sharing of the human spirit; commonly preserved, transmitted and added to by human societies. Just as the total body of science includes the priceless contributions of many great and original minds and would be terribly impoverished if those contributions should be lost; so the total spiritual body of Christianity or of any other great religion has been contributed to by many great, and sometimes original, spirits. The values of science may be largely preserved through literature, but the values of the

74

spiritual bodies of men must be preserved more largely through the contagion of direct, personal association. I believe that in this preservation and transmission the Christian societies of America, in spite of the tragic disservice of theology, and arbitrary indoctrination, have been of great value. It would be well, I believe, if there could be a continuity of these spiritual bodies while they are being freed from the heavy burden of theology and of incongruous metaphysical assumptions by which they are corrupted.

In my search for purpose I would endeavor to enter into the emotional inheritance of this and other spiritual bodies of aspiration, brotherhood, human understanding, and personal commitment to the best that is known. I would constantly examine and critically appraise the contents of these spiritual bodies, for they contain negative elements of pettiness, provincialism, prejudice and vindictiveness, and require intelligent discipline and correction. Among the spiritual bodies the spirit of which I would hope to inherit is the body of science, with its commitment to honest, critical, open inquiry.

I have commented on the disastrous effects of the destruction of the spiritual body of a society. What then shall we say about the spiritual bodies of those religious societies where fine elements of aspiration and purpose have become enmeshed with fantastic theology, medieval or ancient metaphysics, and regimentation of thought and spirit? Here we have one of the dilemmas of our time.

There are a number of promising approaches to this problem. First is from within the religious fellowships. The application of courage and honesty would go a long way. Many a Christian minister doubts what he preaches, and fears to question honestly and fully lest he might come to doubt more. He continues to preach what he thinks is expected of him. He feels that if he should part company with his fellowship he would be socially and professionally an outcast, and economically adrift. Often the intensity of a minister's public as-

75

sertion of his faith is effort to smother doubt as to what would be the result of free, honest inquiry. Having talked with scores of ministers, I do not write simply from general impressions. The internal politics of some denominational hierarchies are so highly elaborated that for a man even to move from his own administrative district means that his hope for advancement is largely ended. Lack of real courage and of intellectual honesty on the part of religious leaders is one of the chief difficulties. Similarly, some active church members who are in business or the professions would find it economically and socially disadvantageous to think honestly and freely in religion, and to act on the results of that thinking.

I know of one inquiring Southern Baptist minister who did some thinking, and began to preach what he believed. His congregation quickly dismissed him. Instead of moving away he remained in the community, lived abstemiously, earned his living by any work he could find, and began to counsel with those who came to him. Though he lives hard, his following is greater than ever before, and is made up, not of indifferent listeners but of persons in various parts of America who are sincerely struggling to find a way of life. Periodical letters and personal conversations take the place of his sermons. He has the joy of spiritual freedom. A few thousand men of such courage and honesty could make a spiritual revolution in America, and could conserve some of the best of the spiritual body of human association while achieving intellectual freedom.

The person who already has broken from intellectual bondage should realize that reason and emotion are equally essential, that living in accord with one's convictions is as important as having right convictions, and that living in a fellowship of aspiration and commitment—a spiritual body— will help him to inherit a great emotional tradition. He may try to become at home in such a spiritual tradition which has

76

stimulated aspiration, aroused a sense of brotherhood and a sharing of life, and has encouraged personal commitment to right living. A liberal fellowship will continue relatively sterile except as a strong and fine spiritual body is developed.

It is most difficult to maintain intellectual freedom while living in a cultural atmosphere or spiritual body which is not free. It is therefore highly important that men of intellectual freedom develop their own spiritual bodies. Here and there are men who will bring the fire with them, and who crave a society of free spirits. I believe that a great spiritual body is more possible among men of free spirit than among those who have been indoctrinated with obsolete mythology and with medieval metaphysics and whose minds have been closed to free inquiry.

Vast numbers of our young people are giving up traditional religious bonds, and are standing for freedom of religious thinking. They tend to see the religious tradition as a single, indivisible pattern, as their priests and ministers have told them it is, and so they throw it all away. They do not see that along with an intolerable regimentation of mind there exists in varying degrees a fellowship of aspiration, brotherhood, commitment and discipline—in total a spiritual body—which is among the greatest treasures of the race. They need help to discriminate between what is obsolete theology and traditional regimentation of thinking, and what is of the very essence of living value. They need the power plant of tested, disciplined, enlightened emotion, directed by the rudder of critical intelligence. A profound disturbance of old faiths and assurances may be essential to that end. My opinion that this is the case leads me to express myself in ways which may cause the giving up of strongly held traditional patterns of thought and belief.

Every great spiritual tradition—or spiritual body—has had its own beginning, often by the very slow accumulation of small increments, sometimes by the tremendous influence

77

of a great spirit, and sometimes by the sustained, intensive commitment of small groups. In nearly every case the apparently new beginning takes over some of the values of the past, as the Christian religion borrowed from the Hebrew and the Greek; or as Buddhism borrowed from Hinduism. Every member of every family and of every other small society can contribute to the quality of its "spiritual body," and thus to the quality of life as a whole. Every person, if he is wise, will seek to possess for himself the best elements of the great spiritual traditions.

VIII THE QUESTION
OF FREEDOM

THERE IS A GENERAL CONVICTION among scientists, and to a considerable degree among men in general, that all phenomena have the interrelation of cause and effect, that everything which occurs has its cause in what previously occurred or existed, and that everything which occurs has some effect. If that is the case, then what justification is there for a belief in freedom of the will? Every reflective person has turned that question over in his mind. Many men feel that they must arrive at a philosophy concerning the subject. It seems to me to be preferable for myself, lacking competence for reaching a conclusion, to admit to myself that I do not know. I have a feeling that if and when men fully clarify this issue it will be found that the question has been falsely stated, and in its conventional form is meaningless. However, I have had some ideas on the subject.

I am inclined to think that "freedom of the will" may be a philosophical abstraction rather than a practical question. It is unimportant in a working sense unless if men should be free they would act more advantageously than otherwise. Only an unwise man would desire to be free in order to injure himself. Our desire to be free rests on the unconscious assumption that if we were free we could improve things. Yet if we are driven by a fate, it seems to be a fate which impels us to try to improve things. We do not know whether we would act differently and yet wisely if we were "free."

Seldom are we explicit as to what we mean by freedom of the will. The cells of my body may have two kinds of freedom. First, there may be a slight individual autonomy within each cell. No two cells would have identically the same life experience, and that small element of individuality may be in

79

some degree self-directing. Sometimes, as in cancer, a group of cells seems to undertake to be free from the total economy of the body. They may kill the body and thereby end their own lives.

Second, the cell as an integral part of a tissue or organ, and then of my body, may be free as my body is free, and so on through larger units of freedom. I may have a limited degree of freedom as an individual, another element of freedom as a member of a partially free community, other degrees of freedom as part of a free city or a free nation, until my greatest degree of freedom would be as an integral part of all existence.

Since in a human society the members have relations with each other and influence each other, complete freedom for one would mean lack of complete freedom for others. Otherwise we should be living, not in a cosmos, but in chaos. Since every part of creation in some degree affects every other part, only the whole can be wholly free. Complete freedom would require omnipotence and omniscience. Only a universal God of all creation, or the whole of creation, could have such freedom.

The fact that I do not have the basis for final judgment on the matter of freedom does not relieve me from the necessity for taking a course of action. I have a feeling that I have a certain limited but significant degree of individual, personal freedom, and that this degree will increase significantly if I use it wisely. My personal freedom may be the power in some degree to modify the whole.

Practical Problems of Freedom. If I assume the course just mentioned there remain practical problems relating to freedom of the same kind as other practical questions of living. In a practical social sense freedom does not refer to any theoretical or absolute right to act without regard to one's social relationships. It refers rather to a practical and fortunate adjustment of human relationships in which the

80

welfare of society as a whole is in harmony with a relatively wide range of self-determination of individual action, and capacity to contribute to the pattern of the whole. In this sense the word freedom is a relative, empirical, practical term, and its meaning depends on circumstances, points of view, and the accepted conventions of society. Particularly it depends on moral or ethical standards prevailing, and on individual desire to live for the total good rather than for one's own private good. In this sense only a religious or ethical society can be a free society.

During the past century the population of the world has doubled and our own has quadrupled. People are closer together. They rub against each other more frequently. The old conditions of relatively independent action cannot continue unchanged. At point after point freedom of action is curtailed. We travel faster, and so are regimented by traffic laws; we are crowded together more and so must have sanitary regulations; our buildings are larger and closer together, so we have building regulations. Speech is supposedly free, but radio bands are limited, so we have a Federal Communications Commission. In a hundred ways we are no longer free to do as we please, but are regimented.

This steadily increasing interrelation of men makes greater interdependence inevitable. To the degree that interdependence is administered by closed minds, arbitrary dogmas, and lack of sensitiveness and consideration for the welfare of others, to that degree only arbitrary force can maintain peace and order, and some approach to totalitarianism is sure. To the degree that free, objective inquiry guides our course, and to the degree that fair play, good will and a sense of human brotherhood motivates our action, to that degree freedom and order can live together. In a practical, social sense freedom is not unrelated separateness of action, but a condition of organic union in which each serves all, and all serve each. Such organic union does not necessarily involve a communal blending of action. Mutual regard may well express itself in care-

81

fully preserving for each person the largest feasible degree of freedom of motion, socially and economically.

This requirement that we adjust ourselves to others is not a bitter necessity, but a desirable condition. Suppose the man who most desires complete freedom from adjustment to others should suddenly find that all other men had perished and that he alone walked the face of the earth. How much joy would he have in that discovery? As W. R. Alger remarked, would he not rush anxiously about, hoping his impression was false and that somewhere he might find a living companion?

It might seem to be a fair definition of practical freedom to say that it is the condition which exists when the outward opportunity of a man corresponds with his inward urge. But that is too simple a statement. A person's own judgment of freedom is not always a measure of the reality. The best way to maintain a despotism is to predetermine that inward urge so that it will give full loyalty to those who exploit it. It might be said that a person is never so much under servitude as when he feels most free. Servitude is never well established so long as it rests chiefly on physical force. Let the tyrant but turn his back, and the slave may rebel. Only when the mind and spirit are brought under servitude, only when the slave accepts his slavery as a heaven-sent blessing, and will fight and die to retain it, can his master rest in peace. Through long ages men of worldly wisdom have realized this, and so the greatest continuing struggle has been for the competitive indoctrination of men's minds. King and priest have become highly skilled in this ancient art.

Always the effort has been to kill the critical faculties, to create in the spirits of men a feeling that the particular doctrines being impressed upon them are excellent above all others, have a unique origin, and provide a sure guide to thought and action. A person effectively indoctrinated has a sense of freedom in loyalty to that indoctrination. Many a good soldier has died "gloriously" in defending the doctrine of the divine right of kings.

82

THE QUESTION OF FREEDOM

The maintenance of freedom is primarily a religious issue. It calls for acting in a spirit of brotherhood, with integrity, considerateness and a spirit of responsibility. It calls, too, for elimination of arbitrary controls and authority in religion, government and economics. Finally, it calls for that sincere commitment to the common good which is the essence of true religion. With increasing population density, increasing interrelation and increasing technology, political, economic and religious authoritarian controls either must decrease or become more arbitrary. Self-interest and strategy will not do. Only freedom of inquiry, mutual regard and great spiritual commitment can bring about the near miracle of freedom in an extremely complex society.

Vows Undermine Freedom. One way by which men may be led to assiduously guard and maintain their own loss of freedom is by encouraging the taking of vows. I use the word "vow" in the usual sense of a promise which precludes the right to re-examine one's position and to change one's course even if deliberate re-examination should convince one that is best. A person taking a vow in effect promises, with respect to the matter involved, to limit free intellectual or spiritual growth. Though his vow may seem unwise in the light of further experience and insight, the "sacred" promise would hold him to his course.

Authoritarian relationships frequently make use of vows. Those who receive or encourage them evidence a willingness to hold the minds and spirits of men in servitude to some mental or emotional attitude which, though sincerely taken, nevertheless may represent but a transitory stage in the growth of the spirit.

The normal life of the spirit demands each day new examination of one's self and of one's purpose, and fresh resolve. Often the tired, baffled spirit is tempted to give up, and by taking formal vows to hand over the direction of his life to the keeping of another, or of an institution, and to find

83

peace by putting an end to intellectual or spiritual search. Yet one way leads to spiritual servitude, the other to life, to freedom, and to unwarped growth. No vow or promise made by my past self is binding if it keeps me from being true to my best present self.

Virtues in their slow, troubled evolution develop many excesses. Self-restraint may become asceticism, thrift may turn into miserliness, and desire for freedom become anarchy. The sense of responsibility, one of man's noblest traits, also may have morbid excess. To mislead or to exploit it, to make it the basis of authoritarian coercion; to capture youthful zeal and aspirations and to bind them irrevocably to a fixed outlook by religious or other vows, is infamous. No longer may an American sell his own body into slavery. Society protects him from that indiscretion. For him to commit his mind through vows or pledges may be no less servitude.

The mind of man should have a right to freedom. (By "right" I mean, not a supernatural or mystical endowment, but recognition and support of a status which accords with good over-all policy.) No emotionally induced or ill-considered pledge I may make to church or state or friends can properly require me to discontinue inquiry into the truth or, within reasonable or necessary limits set by law or society, to refrain from changing my conduct as I change my mind. My sense of responsibility calls for me to assume heavier burdens than any vows. Only as it governs my life can I hope for freedom from external bondage or self-imposed servitude.

No contract is properly inexorable. The validity of each one rests upon the reasonableness of its terms. A contract to give dollars in return for cents would not be sustained in law because the unequal conditions imply some lack of sanity or freedom in its making. If I freely sell for a hundred dollars a mine which later proves to be worth a million, the contract may be good because when all factors, including uncertainty, are taken into account, the exchange is reasonable. In West-

84

ern law the concept has largely disappeared that a vow or pledge or contract inevitably carries obligation or responsibility. Contracts are good when they define relations within reasonable limits of uncertainty. It will be well when promises to one's self or to others have similar authority in morals, when they are used to establish and to define inherently reasonable relationships, and when they have no potency to sustain those which may now or in the future prove to be inherently unreasonable. In both law and morals, understanding of the legitimate functions of contracts brings a greater tendency to enforce the fulfillment of those which are inherently reasonable.

Marriage vows are no exception to the rule that vows are immoral. When people marry they assume one of the chief relationships by which the long struggle for the refinement and mastery of life is carried on. Each party has in large degree the power to make or break the life of the other. If the home fails, then, so far as those persons are concerned, that struggle ends in defeat. The finest human traits are elusive and require exceptional environment such as the home, in which mutual regard, forbearance, affection, and unselfishness have their best chance. Such relationships seldom spring full-grown, but usually develop slowly, often by indomitable determination not to fail. In marriage each gives himself, not by contract or sale, but freely. Recognition of these values and responsibilities constitutes the strongest of ties. Arbitrary bonds, such as marriage vows, may seem to be effective among unthinking people until time can make a more perfect tie, but may they not more probably prevent recognition of the true basis of union? Would not the real reasons for patience and loyalty be more potent than these arbitrary forms? Where separation becomes morally necessary, should it be accompanied by a sense of guilt from broken vows?

It would seem appropriate and helpful for the parties to a marriage to make a clear declaration of the significance of

85

the union and of their intentions as to loyalty, companionship and affection. That would seem to cover all the legitimate purposes of a vow, without its undesirable elements.

Laws, manners, taste, morals and customs may establish useful channels for action. Our animal impulses or imperfect early training may incline us to actions which are out of harmony with standards or ideals of action to which in our best moments we have committed ourselves. Floods of passion or social pressure may powerfully impel us to acts which our calm and deliberate judgment disapproves. Boys or girls of good ethical intent may temporarily find themselves in a period of emotional stress during which a course of action seems good which is in conflict with deliberately formed judgments and standards. Some people undertake to justify vows on the ground that they may hold a person true to his deliberately formed convictions in such periods of emotional stress.

Vows and pledges are not the only way, nor do I believe that they are the right way or the best way, for maintaining standards in time of emotional stress. Moral or ethical counsel and example may teach the general truth that periods of emotional stress do betray deliberately-arrived-at standards and ideals, and such teaching may encourage the habit and the confirmed principle of action that one will not succumb to emotional stress or "temptation," when it is out of harmony with accepted principles and ideals. Where such self-restraint has been developed by teaching and example, it has the increased effectiveness which results when emotional persistence of purpose is in accord with intellectual recognition of the reasonableness of the position taken. A vow or pledge may have only the emotional set to sustain it.

You must not ask that your will or your influence of to-day shall control my mind and my acts of the future, under conditions which neither of us can foresee. The outlook of a moment or of a period must not dominate the conduct of a life.

86

THE QUESTION OF FREEDOM

The Proper Function of "Conditioning." Notwithstanding the destruction of freedom brought about by propaganda and other efforts to establish servitude, we cannot condemn conditioning as an evil in itself. Without it men would still be subhuman animals, lacking speech, society or government. To speak of freedom without recognizing the necessity for education of human habits, emotions and desires is to lack penetration. Human culture itself, its very fibre, consists of the results of the conditioning of men through the centuries so that they will act in certain ways. Stable social order is due to conditioning. Respect for the rights of others becomes an intuitive habit through such influence. How can we distinguish in private choice or in public policy between desirable and undesirable conditioning?

As in many other life issues, no clear and simple rules can be given to guide policy in the matter of conditioning the thinking of people. There are interests which are not controversial, but concerning which it is desirable to have a greater public awareness. It is proper that the public be constantly reminded of the necessity for care in preventing automobile accidents. Similar conditioning is desirable to develop a state of mind which will guard against forest fires. As to broader interests, there are ethical and social standards which have so nearly universal acceptance that the teaching and indoctrination of them will almost surely be in harmony with the long-time judgment of men. Among these standards we may include honesty in dealing with associates, acting for the long-time general good rather than for one's personal good where there is conflict between the two; carrying one's share of the social load; maintaining one's physical and mental health. There are other beliefs, standards and attitudes that are highly controversial. Indoctrination in those is generally of doubtful wisdom. Indoctrination for self-interest or for privilege in conflict with the general good is not justified. Understanding of the nature of indoctrination and other conditioning will help in the formulation of sound policy.

87

IX THE CONTROL OF THE PHYSICAL WORLD[1]

THERE ARE TWO equally important elements in human progress. They are the development of personality and character, and the mastery of the physical world. While working with our personalities and characters is one of the most promising and fundamental ways for fulfilling the possibilities of life, of equal importance and significance is the mastery of the physical world to give men a good environment to live in, and suitable and effective tools. The element of physical mastery commonly has been depreciated by philosophy and religion as of a lower order than spiritual life. Such appraisal is not sound. The two elements are equally imperative to a good life. Man must have a footing on earth, he must have air to breathe, water to drink, food to eat, clothes to wear, shelter from the weather, means of travel and transportation, and tools and materials to use for meeting his needs. He needs mechanical power for great undertakings, microscopes and telescopes to extend his vision, and vast technical equipment and materials to work with. Good will without some degree of these does not produce a good life.

Except for the most primitive of aborigines, men are not content to live in the world as they find it. Only the least developed of peoples rely so much on the "natural" world that they depend for food on the wild fruits and nuts which nature provides. Men make over their own part of that world by clearing the forests and cultivating the land. In some climates

---

[1]Reproduced in part from a talk given at the Indian Institute of Culture, at Bangalore; published in the Calcutta magazine, *Science and Culture*, for February, 1950, and in *The Humanist* magazine, Yellow Springs, Ohio.

they do not depend on natural rain for their crops, but store water for dry weather irrigation. In many ways men make over the "natural" world to suit their needs.

Many other animals control nature and make over their environment in limited ways. Nearly all such abilities are specialized, inherited traits. In man, on the contrary, efforts to control nature and to remake his environment affect nearly every phase of his life, and take numberless forms. Without such mastery of nature the earth would support but a small part of its present human population.

As control over nature increases, men gain increasing security against flood, drouth, famine and disease, and great as have been the gains of men in the past by such controls, the vast possibilities for increasing mastery of nature are barely touched. The security won by that increasing mastery may be of little value unless there is corresponding development of ethical and spiritual qualities. There is no one kind of excellence which by itself will make a good life for individuals or for society. A well proportioned development of all phases of life is desirable. If any one vital element is seriously disregarded, the whole pattern may be greatly reduced in quality. Mastery of nature is not the only condition necessary for a life of dignity and security. Yet it is an essential element, and disregard for such mastery will result in poverty, disease and degradation. The contempt of some religious men for "earthly" things is not justified.

Man should be a harmonious part of the community of nature. When the term "mastery of nature" is used it does not imply that something outside of nature imposes dominance upon it. Rather the expression is used in the way in which we would speak of self-mastery, which does not imply that one part of self domineers over other parts, but that the growing personality achieves integration and internal harmony.

With some people, while any long-established control of nature, such as cultivation of the soil or the building of houses,

89

is accepted, almost as a part of nature, like the building of nests by birds; any recently achieved control seems unnatural and artificial. This difference is in the attitudes of the persons concerned, and not in the processes themselves.

At every step in the history of mankind, increase of mastery of nature has been brought about by three major elements. First, is direct, intimate acquaintance with those elements of nature that are to be mastered. We seldom can either understand or control that with which we are not acquainted. Simple and obvious as this statement seems, failure to realize it has been one of the chief causes of human backwardness.

The second element, important, but not always present, is understanding. Only as there is capacity and desire to understand, to see what has meaning and why, and to see how things are related to each other, can increasing control of nature be best brought about. Quite frequently understanding is inadequate or absent, and increased control has been the result of trial-and-error fumbling, or even of sheer accident. There should be enough understanding to recognize a desirable new situation. The other animals and primitive men have first-hand intimate acquaintance with nature, but with little understanding. Understanding is gradually developed in society, and is passed on from generation to generation. Only that intelligence which is supported by accumulated social wisdom is adequate for the mastery of nature. That is, wide-ranging education, either formal or informal, as well as ranging intelligence, is essential to the most effective and progressive mastery.

Third, increase of mastery of nature requires skill of hand, ear, and eye. The most brilliant and penetrating theory is without effect in controlling the environment and in remaking our world until appropriate skill of hand, ear and eye have done their part.

Understanding and familiarity with the physical world, acting by themselves, produce the scientist. Skill of hand and

90

eye, and familiarity with tools and with the phases of the physical world being dealt with, produce the craftsman or technician. Finally, these various activities are most effective for making desirable changes in our environment when they are associated with each other. Just as men do not cooperate most efficiently if they are strangers, but only when they are intimately acquainted and have learned to work in unison, so brain and hand do not cooperate effectively if they are nearly strangers. Cooperation is best when they have developed such habitual coordination as that of the hands and mind of a master of the violin who expresses his mind and soul as he plays a musical instrument with his hands. Such coordination of mind and hand as a rule results only from a lifetime of the practice of coordination.

I am of the opinion that in nearly all civilized countries certain attitudes have prevailed which have interfered with the growing mastery of nature. Until two or three hundred years ago Europe was largely in the same retarded condition as India. The sudden development of control of nature which has taken place in the Western world has not resulted from anything new being added to the earth, nor from any sudden increase in the mental ability of men, but followed liberation from certain kinds of bondage of mind and spirit which had kept men largely helpless. Even today that liberation of the western mind has only begun. There are two attitudes which, in my opinion, have interfered seriously with that increasing mastery of nature. One of these is the social caste system and the other is the common philosophic attitude of retreat from objective reality. Curiously, these two attitudes have somewhat the same adverse effect on man's mastery of his environment.

Europe has had its caste system. Men of different hereditary classes or castes become skilled in their own fields, but seldom achieve familiarity and mastery of the work of other castes. Because some of them provide the philosophers and reflective thinkers while others developed skill of hand

91

and eye in craftsmanship, while perhaps still others provided skill in administration and management, there has tended to be a lack of that union of reflection and of execution and of union of mind and hand with intimate acquaintance with materials, which are necessary to advance our control over nature. The man of scholarship and reflective thinking commonly has lacked effective familiarity with the physical world. On the other hand, both the administrator and the skilled craftsman lacked much of the intellectual, cultural inheritance and of the philosophic outlook. Thus because under the social caste system intellectual development and reflective thought tended to be divorced from practical management and from craftsmanship, the person of reflective thought did not have the necessary practical skill to remake his environment, while the practical manager and the skilled craftsman did not inherit the tradition of ranging mind and philosophic reflection which produce mental pictures of the new world men need to fulfill their possibilities. The simple fact of this lack of coordination of mind and hand has had a profound effect both on philosophy and theology, and on practical life. But for the fact that for a thousand years medieval Europe had its caste system, and but for its philosophic retreat from reality, the present age of growing mastery of nature might have dawned on Europe two thousand years ago.

It is desirable again to emphasize that the kind of mastery which controls the physical environment, and makes over the natural world to suit man's purpose, definitely requires both intimate first-hand acquaintance with the elements to be mastered, and the disciplined and practical skill of eye and hand which makes possible the effective manipulation of tools and materials. Every step in the actual control of man's environment has called for such intimate acquaintance and for such skill with physical things.

Now it is a usual characteristic of the speculative philosopher that his attention is directed, not to the objective world

92

about him, but inward upon his own thoughts and mental processes. When he reads, it is commonly the writings of other men whose thoughts were similarly directed.[2]

Because the philosopher's mind is turned inward, he is generally unskilled and inept in handling physical things. With doubtless many individual exceptions, such as Spinoza, the spectacle maker, this has been characteristic of philosophers from time immemorial, at least until recently. Simple and incidental as that fact may seem, its natural and almost necessary results are far-reaching and momentous, on the one hand to philosophy and on the other hand to man's degree of control of his physical environment.

Scarcely any course of action which could be devised short of solitary confinement in an empty cell would so induce to ineptitude in dealing with objective reality as does that of the speculative philosopher in turning his mind away from the phenomenal world and centering his attention on the world of abstract ideas. Not only is he ill-equipped for the mastery of nature, but he is not greatly interested in such mastery.

And here is a significant result. The philosopher's personal helplessness before objective nature almost inevitably reacts upon his outlook. In his mind that helplessness which he experiences in himself comes to be one of the given facts of life. It seems to him to be but an instance of the impotence of man before nature. That helplessness seems so completely obvious that it seldom comes into question in philosophical

———

[2]No broad generalization, such as "speculative philosopher," is wholly sound. Many philosophers, ancient and modern, have been concerned with the nature of the material world, and with its mastery. Democritus, Archimedes, and Lucretius are examples from the ancient world, as John Dewey and others are of the recent past. Notwithstanding the many such cases, this characterization of speculative philosophy in general seems to be valid.

discussion, and seems to require no argument. To question it in any but small matters seems to him to be fantasy. Generalizing his own helplessness as a universal and inevitable helplessness of man before the natural world, that helplessness becomes an inherent part of his philosophy.

There is an impulse in man, as in every living thing, to achieve completion of an ideal pattern. For instance, every tree that grows has such an impulse to realize an ideal. Every twig and every leaf which it produces is in response to that impulse to perfection. Such impulse never has full expression because perfect fulfillment is sure to be more or less prevented by adverse circumstance, and perhaps by inner conflict or incongruity within the pattern. Man as an animal shares with all plant and animal life this impulse to fulfill an ideal type. So far as his physical body is concerned, he is like plants and other animals in that he has but limited choice as to what that bodily pattern will be. His physical type is substantially determined before his birth, and "which of you by taking thought can add one cubit unto his stature?"

But man has qualities of mind and spirit which are scarcely if at all evident in lower animals. His mind also has cravings to fulfill ideal patterns, and these patterns are not dictated to him before birth to the same extent as is the ideal pattern for his body. To some degree he seems to be free to create his own ideal patterns in his mind or spirit, or to adopt those strongly presented to him.

This innate drive to fulfill a pattern or ideal attaches itself to, or serves to promote, whatever pattern is approved by emotion or intelligence. I recall a young Mexican who turned from being an ardent Catholic to become an ardent communist. The innate drive which served one pattern served also to help fulfill the other.

Freedom to create, or by influence, or by exploration and comparison, to select, one's own ideal pattern of mind and spirit is far from complete. A man's range of choice is partly limited by his biological inheritance. There are also elements of compulsion in social tradition, in governmental requirements, in religious indoctrination, in climatic conditions, in economic circumstance, and in the prevailing mores. Yet, it seems that the individual may to some degree create his own ideal pattern. By observation and reflective thinking he can give consideration to logical relationships of cause and effect. Sometimes bursts of imagination or of creative intuition or insight make their contributions.

The objectives or mental pictures to which men commit their life efforts vary greatly in social value. Some of these call for influencing the motives of men toward peace on earth and good will toward men. Some are concerned with personal satisfaction or aggrandizement, often regardless of the effect on the lives of others. Dictators, exploiters and self-seekers of many kinds develop such mental pictures and try to fulfill them. Some men have aims of increasing man's power over nature, of subduing the earth and making it over so that it will be more suitable for fulfilling human need.

It is a characteristic of men that they do not easily accept defeat. As they find fulfillment impossible in one direction they turn to another. The philosopher, seemingly helpless before the vast tyranny of the physical world, turns to the world of speculative ideas. Unable to drive a nail or to plant a field, he comes to have his interests and to make his home in the world of his speculations. In that other world actualities do not enter to mar his "ideal" structure. The more that mental picture is beyond test by the senses, then the more immune it is to injury, and the more he feels securely at home in it. Compared with the vast sweep of his mind, how trivial and mean are the efforts of men to drain a swamp, to build a house, even to assemble an empire! Craving a sense of reality and validity for the world of ideas he has created, he comes to view his world of speculation, which cannot be tested by the senses, as the world of reality, while the physical world

95

around him he calls illusion. Has he not, in effect, found escape from reality? Is not this flight from the phenomenal world a sin of philosophy against mankind?

There is not necessarily any purity or refinement in escape from objectivity. A philosopher may carry over into the realm of abstract ideas the arrogant positiveness of a dominant caste. Purity of spirit may therefore be more commonly found among the lowly than among those who flee from the objective world to that of abstract speculation.

Without the humbling discipline which comes from relating one's thinking to objective reality the philosopher may become arbitrary, irresponsible and capricious. The philosopher who lives in a world of speculative abstractions must also live in the phenomenal world. Since the two worlds are often incongruous, the habit develops of living with and accepting incongruity as natural. To carry truth and falsehood together comes to be called tolerance. Incompatibles come to live together in his mind, creating inherent disharmony, a condition not favorable to development of a great integrity of spirit, or a great ethic. Once that incongruity is accepted, it is a relatively short step to accept the theological absurdities which he finds current.

Even when speculative theology or philosophy calls men to action, unless there is a live belief in the possibility of remaking the world to serve the needs of life, the action called for may be only a sort of ceremonial, a sacrament required by the gods, like baptism for the Christian, rather than a process of remaking the environment. Only out of faith in the value of purposeful action can action become effective or ennobled.

As the philosopher's influence spreads, the attitude tends to prevail in society that the world of speculation, of patterns and theories beyond the test of objective experience, is important, while the physical world is relatively unimportant. Is not the western world only gradually liberating itself from that belief? When men come to give first allegiance to a world

96

of speculation which is beyond objective examination, the increasing mastery of the objective world, the progressive re-making of man's environment to suit his needs, slows down or stops. In such case, the latent mental, spiritual and physical capacities for mastering the physical world are still present in men, but belief in the possibility of such mastery, and the spirit to undertake it, are gone. Whenever speculative philosophy in its flight from objective reality, becomes dominant, then man's mastery of his objective world declines.

Such a decline in the habit of mastering nature and controlling the environment has taken place in India. There, where this product of speculative philosophy has been fixed in the minds of the people as perhaps nowhere else on earth, and over a long period, and where more than anywhere else a purely speculative view of life is held to be superior to a mastery of the objective world, what do we find as to man's relation to nature? The tools men use for living in India are more primitive and less productive than in any other civilized country. A day of a man's life in labor will produce less of the physical goods men live by than in any other civilized country. The life span is shorter than in any other such country. Poverty is more general and more extreme. Disease is more prevalent. Fifty thousand men from a country half-way around the world, which did not despise mastery of nature, for centuries held in subjection a population of hundreds of millions. Servitude of spirit was ingrained in a great people.

Because the intellectual leadership of India concerned itself with speculative philosophy which did not give major attention to remaking the world, the man of action was not provided with a great pattern for his life. Following the conventional patterns of men of action, he became a great military conqueror. With great power to control circumstances he built himself a kingdom, built it on human blood, or by the servitude of many men built himself a palace which cut him off from the common life. If the concern of thinking men had been the mastery of nature for the benefit of the common

97

life, then a great ideal pattern of action would have existed to receive the loyalty of men of action. If we ignore esoteric criteria so private that they cannot be communicated to others, the fruits of speculative philosophy have not been glorious.

✓   ✓   ✓

The philosopher makes vast generalizations which in his mind describe the underlying nature of things and include all the world. For instance, there is the concept of "evil" as an inherent element in the nature of the world. Before such a universal as "evil" man seems hopeless. What can he do against what seems to be the very nature of existence? Yet, in fact the abstract idea of "evil" is a philosophic creation.

Suppose that instead of being a speculative philosopher dealing with vast speculative generalizations, such as "evil," the man of insight is a practical person, seeing what he actually sees. What he actually has experience with is not the abstract generalization "evil," but certain specific evils. Concerning some of these he may not be entirely helpless. One evil he observes is starvation. He can turn his attention to better varieties of crops, better methods of cultivation, more certain water supply. Perhaps there is overpopulation. He may study population balance and develop elements of population policy. Disease is rampant. He can study the causes of classes of disease and of particular diseases, and the nature of the human body that is subject to disease, and little by little he may master disease.

Such an objective approach to life has spiritual quality. At the Buddhist temple at Sarnath there are murals depicting incidents in the life of Buddha. One of these pictures the master bathing the body of a man ill with dysentery. Today, nearly 2500 years later, that disease is probably as prevalent in India as when Buddha performed this act of mercy and brotherhood. Would there have been any less a spiritual tradition if through the years a band of devoted men had studied the nature and causes of dysentery so that it might be eliminated? In some large areas of the western world dysentery has been almost eliminated by men who did not speculate on the abstract concept of evil, but did study the nature of dysentery.

Think of the great Buddhist university of Nalanda, lasting through nearly a millennium with 8000 to 10,000 students. The endowment of this university consisted of scores or hundreds of villages whose inhabitants must spend their lifetimes at labor so these students could study religion and philosophy. What if, instead of speculative philosophy, dealing largely with subjects beyond experimental inquiry, the university had been engaged in teaching how to master physical circumstance and to remake men's environment!

If we should escape from the concept of the helplessness of man in the objective world and should bend our energies on the mastery of nature, what fields might be covered and what gains might we expect! Suppose we try to picture what might have happened through the centuries if the remarkable minds which gave form and content to Indian speculative philosophy had instead seen the hope of mankind as to be achieved through the mastery of phenomenal circumstance and the rebuilding of the world about us. Let us include in the world which is subject to rebuilding not only wood and stone, but also the make-up of man and society, so far as that remaking is possible within the range of human skill and purpose. Thus we may include objective ethics, social policy, economic policy, medical practice, psychiatry, population policy, and eugenics, as well as more obvious fields such as biology, chemistry, physics, engineering, forestry and agriculture.

As a first requirement for rebuilding our objective world there is needed the objective, critical mind. One of the greatest needs of humanity is, not to be taught by arbitrary authority what is good, beautiful and true, but to be encouraged to inquire. *Teaching by arbitrary authority puts the mind to*

99

sleep. Inquiry keeps it awake. The great teachers of the past may have felt that the truths they had won were so precious, and the minds to whom they would transmit them were so immature, that only by authoritative teaching could the great message be preserved. That attitude might be called the original great mistake of the teacher, since it set up a process that is inherently deadening to the spirit of inquiry. Had the attitude of mutual inquiry been nurtured, then those who were taught would in time surpass their teachers. A renewing and creative process would be under way. Nothing would be so sacred as to be immune from that process.

In the field of man's protection from physical disaster, the last few centuries in the western world have made great headway. Many sources of physical catastrophe can be removed, and others can be made increasingly harmless. Earthquakes cannot be prevented, but we can know just where they are likely to occur, and can largely prevent damage by them. The ocean hurricane cannot as yet be stopped, but it can be somewhat foretold and avoided. On the whole in technically advanced countries physical catastrophe of nature is coming to be one of the minor dangers, and every year the range of possibility for removing such insecurity is greater.

Throughout human history the greatest source of tragedy, aside from man's inhumanity to man, has been economic need. Today hunger and poverty are no longer beyond technical control. The most thickly settled regions on earth could have food in abundance from their own production if the most effective methods we know were generally in use. This is true even though our knowledge of soil, climate and crops is in its infancy. The technical possibilities of feeding the world will probably always run far ahead of the increase of population. Most professional estimates of possible food supply assume production by methods that are far short of the best we know.

Population policy, with limitations of population density, is necessary, but for hygienic, esthetic, cultural and spiritual,

100

rather than for economic, reasons. Men live best with adequate space and freedom of movement. Too dense population tends to lower the quality of life. Overcrowding and its results may be a source of human tragedy. Here too, critical research may replace blind dogma, and vague impression may be replaced by sound population policy, and so may decrease or remove a source of tragedy.

Disease also has been a vast source of frustration. More progress in the cure and prevention of disease has been made in the past century than in all preceding history, and progress was never more rapid than now. Had critical inquiry in this field been active for the past two thousand years it is probable that tragedy from disease would now be rare.

Mental illness as well as physical, so much on the increase in our uncoordinated modern life, is subject to understanding and control and prevention. Although knowledge of mental health is in its infancy, it seems reasonable to look forward to a time when the tragedy of mental ill health will be a rarity.

Partly, the freedom we foresee from mental as well as physical frustration will come from the study and practice of eugenics. Through the coming years eugenic research, education and policy may lead to rapid and sustained improvement of human quality, and tragedy from inadequacy of human genetic inheritance may largely disappear.

Among the chief sources of human tragedy have been the false traditions, myths, mores and customs with which men have been burdened. Here, too, free inquiry and penetrating search, along with intelligent education, can remove a great burden.

And so in the fields of social, economic and political organization, if we withdraw our attention from evil as a philosophical abstraction, and center it upon some particular evils we can help to remove or on some particular promises of human fulfillment we can hope to achieve, the whole color and flavor of life may change.

101

In this process of mastering the problems of life item by item, through disciplined observation, reflective thinking on what we have observed, skill of eye and of hand in doing what needs to be done, and experienced skill of administration in bringing about necessary changes, will men some time come to a stone wall which will prevent any further progress? Perhaps there is no impassable wall. Perhaps as we do the best we can the way will always open ahead, for mastery of the material world is the process of finding or of making a way.

The speculative mind may think, "But suppose man achieves all you have dreamed. Suppose you eliminate most of the natural catastrophes and conflicts, drought and famine; suppose you do all that. And suppose also, through your psychologists, doctors, and your good education you get rid of superstition and mythology, get rid of the warps and twists of mind, and clear away all those specific evils. What has been gained in the end? For without doubt our planet itself will cease to sustain life. Man's day, and the day of all terrestrial life, will be past." Such statements, I think, are unscientific sensationalism. Think how slight was the power man had over his world a brief two hundred years ago! If someone had said, "The time will come when men will fly half-way around the world," would he not have been considered a freak? In the late nineteen-twenties I talked with some of the ablest scientists of America as to the possibility of men ever using atomic energy. One of them said, "It is thought about, but the conditions are so fundamentally against it that it is probably only a dream. It probably can never happen that we will get the energy of the atom. It is probably one of the ultimate impossibilities."

Recently I read a considerable number of world-famous utopias, and observed the "wild" flights of fancy of the authors as they pictured the wonderful achievements of man in the ages to come. It is interesting that the real achievements of men have far outstripped most of these wild fancies

102

of a few decades or a few centuries ago. So, in regard to the ultimate destiny of man, we are unsafe in putting limits upon it. Is it not possible that, even before man has made himself fit to be an immigrant to new lands, he will have the skill and power to travel to other planets and to other solar systems? Our planet may serve as an incubator or pilot plant to get man started on his way. A common toad must hatch its eggs in the water as did the aquatic forebears from which it evolved, but when the tadpole stage is past the young can range over the earth in search of new ponds. So the human species, perhaps, may use this planet for a starting-place. Philosophers and theologians make no apology for letting their minds range on speculative abstractions where they have no basis in evidence. In contrast, to assume far-reaching physical conquest we need only to extrapolate from first-hand experience. That is dangerous, but not necessarily unproductive.

If we can take hold of the work before us—the disease, the poverty, the waste land that will support more people; if we can affect the causes of strife; if we can turn our attention to see, not evil as a universal abstraction, but specific evils which we can have some part in removing; if we push back the barriers of life, and enlarge the range of human possibilities; our efforts may have enduring value, and may be schooling for yet greater conquests. The philosopher's disregard of the physical world has been an error. We need not have less of spiritual life, but it can find expression in mastery of our world, rather than in flight from its problems. By mastery of our world, I repeat, is not meant dominance of one part over another, but integration of growing human purpose with the objective world of which we may be harmonious elements in the community of nature.

Perhaps there is no predetermined road that man must travel. Perhaps the possible courses which life can take are endless, and perhaps we can have a part in deciding which way we shall take. It is left to us to explore and inquire as to

103

which ways are more excellent and which less excellent. Science must deal with values. For instance, if we examine our codes of ethics objectively, such examination may take us into chemistry, biology, psychology, economics and sociology. Dr. Abraham Myerson commented on the fact that the destruction of certain glands by a gunshot wound may change a man's entire character. We would do well to know what are the actual causes and effects of various elements of conduct. The world is full of obsolete or mistaken moralities, held on arbitrary authority. Suppose we begin to look at these, examine them as to how they actually affect human life. In a world of growing understanding and purpose, ethical standards and understanding also must grow or disaster may follow, as is threatened now by obsolete standards of national sovereignty, which may mean national irresponsibility. Many elements of conventional ethical codes are obsolete both because they include mistaken or obsolete standards, and because they omit standards vital to the well-being of life.

Both the western world and the Indian world have looked upon the weight and burden of life as something beyond our control. According to that view we can alleviate suffering for each other here and there in a spirit of love and brotherhood, like the Buddha washing the man with dysentery, but in the total, we are helpless before physical fate. We need a new kind of faith, the faith that man can master his objective world. If we can have that faith, then spiritual quality can find motivation. Each day's work of every man, be his ability small or great, can be adding to the quality of life. He will not be believing in a vale of tears for which the best hope is escape into a world of speculation. He will be engaged in a promising adventure, with possibility of unending increase in value. The concept of progress is not an illusion.

Mankind is on a great adventure in a world of objective reality. Perhaps it is a real adventure. There may be risk of failure. We do not know the time clock of the world. The

104

time available for mastery may not be unlimited. Perhaps how you and I live will make a substantial difference to the outcome. Perhaps the precious time we have spent in building speculative fantasies that are beyond the range of objective inquiry is largely wasted. Does not the world of objective nature call us to great responsibilities as well as to vast opportunities?

I do not see that the physical exigencies of life should incline me to pessimism. Any religion which omits or neglects mastery of the physical world is inadequate and mistaken.

Proportion in Living. The mastery of the objective world is on a par, in importance, significance and value, with the mental and spiritual development of men. The two elements of development are necessary to each other, and neither can go very far without help of the other. In a well-proportioned life they will have equal dignity and loyalty. The key to this statement is the expression "well proportioned." That should be the aim of education and religion and of our life as a whole.

Somewhat as India has fallen short by preoccupation with introspection and speculative philosophy, so present-day America is going to an extreme in its preoccupation with mastery of physical materials, while self-mastery and clarification of purpose is being ignored or neglected. We seem to assume that we can make up for their lack by producing more goods and by further near miracles of material invention and creation. The assumption of American politics and diplomacy, that we can win the respect of the world with power, machines and money, is rapidly losing us friends over the world, just as undue reliance on them is losing us character and quality at home.

It never is safe to try to compensate for one extreme by going to another. One frequently meets Americans who are oppressed by the prevailing disregard for character and purpose, and who incline to repudiate the entire pattern of our

105

mastery of the physical world. I believe they are mistaken. The advance which the present time has made in the mastery of our environment, and in the use of the material world for meeting human need, will, I believe, stand out in history as one of the great liberating achievements of the race. Respect for such mastery will be looked upon as a great advance in human outlook. What we need is not to belittle or to disparage that development, but to give greatly increased emphasis to ethics, character and purpose.

X MY INCENTIVES

SOMETIMES we have beautiful spring mornings when the air is fresh, the flowers are out, and we are caught in the stimulus of spring. We say to ourselves, "This is good. If life were like this it would be worth living." Everyone has experiences when life is good; sometimes longer, sometimes shorter, sometimes almost unalloyed, sometimes mixed with pain. So far as I can see, all humanity has been searching and struggling for increase of value; that is, for increase of experience which to the person concerned seems better to have than not to have, and for decrease of experience which it seems to him it is better not to have than to have.

Sensitivity to the possibilities of the quest of life gives me my major incentives or motives, and I think it can give motivation to most men. Incentives are greatly affected by conditioning. The incentives or motivation to which we were born and reared may by accident of circumstance have been good, bad or indifferent. We are not bound to live in servitude to those conditions.

One of the great truths of life is that, given the seed of a motive to achieve significance for one's life, a man can remake his motives or incentives according to the best and largest pattern he can conceive. To say of any aim or purpose, "It does not interest me, it leaves me cold," is not a statement of what one's life interests must be, but only what they happen to be today. What they will be in the future is largely of our own making. The important question to ask of any pattern of life is not, "Does it interest me?" but rather, "Is it inherently valid and important?" The education of interest and desire is essential to effective living.

We have seen men whose interests lay almost solely in their animal appetites, and we have seen life go stale with them. We have seen parents with their interests centered almost wholly on their children. If the children are well, thriving and honored, then though the parents are fading in vitality and in capacity for animal satisfactions, they continue to have interest and joy in their children. But they do not have the children's fate in their hands. The children may die or be failures. Similarly, we may live for our town, our community or our favorite institution. Yet here again we do not have full control. We have seen men pour out their lives for some institution, and then be disillusioned. But if our hearts are in the success of the human adventure or the adventure of life as a whole, if our chief joy comes in contributing to its fruition, that is a joy which is not easily taken away. I may be dying, my children may die, the institution to which I have given my loyalty may lose its character; but if the way I have lived and what I have done has helped the prospects of the human adventure, I am largely immune to a sense of frustration, unless my mental faculties fail me.

Loyalty to the adventure of life as a whole is not an abstraction, but finds expression in many loyalties, all of them, however, subordinate to the over-all purpose. I should have loyalty to my family, my town, my country, but not to "my country, right or wrong." My loyalty to my children will not go to the length of accumulating an estate for them by carrying on a business of promoting the use of opium in Africa. The more immediate loyalty must be subordinate to and be conditioned by my over-all objective.

It is from this background of thinking that I have tried to determine my incentives and motives. I have come to feel much less keenly a craving for self-perpetuation than for the success of mankind in its search for enduring values. That quest of humanity is "where my treasure is" and "where my heart is also." Not that self-interest, immediate and long-range, has disappeared, but that I see it as subordinate to and disciplined by the larger aim. This is not an attitude acquired in age. It has been my aim and my religion for more than

108

three quarters of my life. As a practical working motive it was somewhat less vividly in my attention, though not absent, during the years when I was struggling to get an economic foothold.

One can have a continuing strong purpose even though he fails in it over and over. No such fundamental undertaking is easily or quickly fulfilled. Most lives, when measured by their aims, are largely failures; yet where there has been a sincere effort to live in the interest of the whole of life, there will be fragments and residues of achievement, and it is out of such fragments and residues that human culture, the greatest treasure of the race, has been built. To live so that one's feeling of reality and his joy come from the prospect of the human adventure, that is living indeed. For a person who has that incentive and motivation, the dilemma of conflict between living for immediate ends and living for the long-time success of the human adventure is largely resolved.

I do not want to hold a philosophy of life because it is comforting or because it gives me strong incentive. I want to hold a philosophy because I have arrived at it in the course of a sincere search for the truth. Then I would build my interest and incentive to support that view.

Even should my hope and purpose not seem fully adequate, I would rather have a purpose which seems to me to accord with the nature of things than to have a dream of what would be more adequate, but which did not rest on the nature of things as they are, or as they might be with the help of the creative imagination and effort of men. To me my hopes and aims seem more reasonable and also more adequate than those of the conventional theologians or the mystics.

In two respects, so far as I can see, the outcome of the quest for enduring values is uncertain. First, the whole adventure might fail, either through some cosmic circumstance or as a result of some ultimate human stupidity which would eliminate the race. Second, among the vast number of possibilities of endlessly varied degrees of excellence, less than the best might be determined upon and achieved.

As a perhaps fanciful example of the first possibility, suppose it to be possible that at some time in the future an atomic energy war, or a war by spreading disease or poison, might end the human race. If in the meantime ethical and emotional growth were great enough, the growth of good will might forestall such a catastrophe, and the powers of men might be used instead to fulfill great possibilities. If human character and purpose had been at their best for the past thousand years, the present world dilemma of fear, suspicion and hate would not exist. Informed purposefulness is so rare that your life and mine may be significant, if small, elements in determining what course is taken. In such case it may be a highly practical matter how we live. Although atomic war is in the public mind, and therefore serves as an example, there probably are other causes of failure of the human quest which are of more serious portent.

Somewhat the same reasoning holds as to the possibility that at some time in the future the earth will no longer serve as a base for the human adventure. Suppose that we should know definitely that in the year 3000 A.D. the earth would no longer be habitable. How would that affect our present life? The churchmen would set days of prayer. Philosophers might find solace in Platonic idealism. Scientists and technicians would begin to do intensive research on possibilities of migration to a setting that would sustain life. Deeply religious men, realizing that effectiveness is an outcome of character, would endeavor to encourage refinement of the minds and spirits of men so that they would work together in harmony and thereby increase the possibility of a successful outcome of the crisis. Men of religion, men of science, and practical administrators working together would have the hopes of men in their hands. In whatever direction danger may lie, acceleration of the development of human quality and character probably will increase the chance of mastering it.

110

As to the second type of possible failure, that of achieving less than the best possible, every person by the quality of his life can increase the rate of realization of value, and can contribute to the possibility of greater excellence. We do not know what exigencies await the human adventure. It is highly probable that whatever those exigencies may be, whether they are surmounted successfully and how successfully will be determined in large part by the extent to which men put the best they have into the undertaking. In any case, the extent to which life will consist of individual tragedies and frustrations on the one hand, or on the other hand of fulfillment and a sense of well-being, probably will depend largely on how you and I and others handle our own lives. That realization supplies me with my incentive.

The chemist in his laboratory decides that he wants a compound of very specific and unusual characteristics. He discovers, by calculation and by trial, the conditions under which it may be brought into existence. These conditions may include very closely measured amounts of exceptionally pure portions of various rare chemical substances which may seldom or never be found in natural association; brought together in chemically inert containers under very closely controlled conditions of temperature, pressure, light, electric charge and time—such a combination of conditions as probably never has occurred on the earth, and perhaps never in the universe. By such methods the chemist produces substances useful or interesting to him, which perhaps never have existed on earth. His intelligent, disciplined, experienced purposefulness enables him to do such things.

Similarly, through intelligent, disciplined, purposeful inquiry men can come to considerable understanding, of the nature of life, of what conditions would give it near maximum value, and of how those conditions may be realized. The very complexity of the human body, of human culture, and of the physical environment, increase the range of such possibilities.

111

Life may be guided toward one or more of innumerable directions, developments, attitudes, and combinations of elements. It seems very highly probable that among these some, or probably very many, may be of such a nature as to make life a highly desirable experience. It is my opportunity to share in the effort to insure that mankind will discover and realize such desirable possibilities. My awareness of the existence of that opportunity harmonizes with and reinforces my biological incentive to live.

In maintaining that incentive I accept the support of the innate drive of life to survive. That drive to survive—or "will-to-live"—is not necessarily conclusive evidence that life has purpose or value, any more than is the fact that water flows downhill conclusive evidence that it is of value to water to flow downhill. Life which has will-to-live is more apt to survive and to continue than life which does not have the will-to-live. So long as life exists, the drive to survive or will-to-live will be present as an almost inevitable result of biological selection, whether or not life has value.

I can reason that if the will-to-live is a drive with no relation to value, then the very process of natural selection might keep men blind to that fact. For some men to believe that life is without possible value, whether or not that belief should be true, would tend to reduce the will-to-live of such men, and thus reduce their prospects for survival. For some men to believe that life does have value, even if that belief should be false, would increase the will-to-live of such men, and so their chance for survival. A very strong case could be made for the probability that if life should be valueless men in general never would find it out, because whoever did find it out would tend to lose the will-to-live, and so would lose survival prospects as compared with those who would think that life does have value. If a person is trying to be honest with himself in facing realities he will not avoid such questions.

112

MY INCENTIVES

Albert Schweitzer of Europe and West Africa—musician, philosopher, physician, surgeon, missionary—is a person whom I greatly admire. He wrote frequently of the will-to-live, with honesty and effort at objectivity which calls for my admiration and respect. However, his point of view on this subject is one I cannot accept, and I can perhaps best clarify my own attitude by quoting him and indicating where I do not agree. No brief quotations can transmit his honesty of thinking, but the following may convey a hint of his convictions. Most of the passages quoted here and in a succeeding chapter are taken from *Albert Schweitzer, an Anthology*, published by the Beacon Press, Boston.

> Ethics is in fact reverence for the will-to-live both within and without my own personality. . . .
> To affirm life is to deepen, to make more inward, and to exalt the will-to-live. . . .
> My knowledge of the world is a knowledge from the outside and must always remain incomplete. The knowledge derived from my will-to-live is, on the contrary, direct, and goes back to the secret springs of life as life exists in itself. The highest knowledge is thus to know that I must be true to the will-to-live. This it is which plots the course for me that I must follow through the night without a chart.

Schweitzer speaks of "the absolute ethics of the will-to-live," and of "affirmation of the world, that is to say, affirmation of the will-to-live."

I am disinclined to attribute supernatural or mystical significance to whatever has a reasonable and natural explanation. It seems to me that the will-to-live is a perfectly natural, almost inevitable, outcome of natural selection. Many arctic animals—rabbits, foxes, bears, owls—in winter change their outside covering to white. On white snow a rabbit with dark fur would be conspicuous, and easy prey. A fox with dark

113

fur could be easily seen moving over white snow, and there would be good chance of escaping it. With the members of each species, selection tends to help to the survival of the particular line of the particular species involved, of the "bad" fox as well as of the "good" rabbit.

The will-to-live seems a natural, almost inevitable, device to further survival; the life in which it is strong will be much more apt to endure than the life in which it is weak. It would seem that the will-to-live of itself may be just a technique for survival, more universal and important, but otherwise of the same general character as other techniques. It may be that life has originated many times, only to lack some characteristic necessary for survival. If some form had the will-to-live, while other forms did not, it is easy to see which form would most probably survive. As a hint that the presence of the will-to-live is not conclusive proof of its value, does not Buddhism picture the overcoming of the will-to-live as among the highest of all aims? I incline to see the will-to-live as a fact to understand, rather than as a mystery to worship.

As an illustration of Schweitzer's effort to be honest in his thinking, the following from his writings is interesting:

> Certainly man's life can hardly be considered the goal of the universe. Its margin of existence is always precarious. . . . The Creative Force does not concern itself about preserving life. It simultaneously creates and destroys. Therefore, the will-to-live is not to be understood within the circle of Creative Force. Philosophy and religion have repeatedly sought the solution by this road; they have projected our will to perfection into nature at large, expecting to see its counterpart there. But in all honesty we must confess that to cling to such a belief is to delude ourselves.

I have tried to present to myself without reservation the possibility that the will-to-live is not evidence of value of living, but may be just a method—perhaps a blind method—

114

which naturally emerges in the process of natural selection. In specific instances nature has deceived her creatures with false optimism, seemingly because it conduces to survival. For instance, it is common for unsophisticated youth to believe that the getting of a mate will largely insure felicity. So strong is this expectation that observation to the contrary in life around them does not undeceive them. Perhaps the will-to-live is a similar case.

What is my response to this line of thinking? First, even if it should be true that the innate drive for survival has been purposeless, except for the blind purpose of survival, and is not aimed at achieving value, I am not bound by that purposelessness. Man can achieve or create aim or purpose, and from among the near infinity of possibilities for human life, may achieve value. Should it be true that man is a cosmic, purposeless accident, as would seem to have been the case with many millions of species which became extinct without descendants, then that accident in his particular case has resulted in the possibility of purposefulness. In acting with purpose it seems probable that he may give direction to events, and may be the cause of far-reaching and significant events. Among the near infinity of possibilities for human life men may bring about the emergence of such conditions that life will be predominantly an experience of value.

The second element of my response is that if I find no conflict between my innate will-to-live and my conscious purpose, then I shall welcome the help of that innate drive, just as I welcome the innate appetite for food to help keep me nourished. Moreover, I believe that the general course I have set for myself, including commitment to free inquiry, will tend to the increase of objectivity. Capacity for objectiveness will enable others to reappraise the situation at any time, so my course is not burning any bridges to inquiry.

Where men have postulated an all-powerful purposeful benevolence which sets desirable ends for men and guides them toward it, they face the dilemma that life seems to have

115

about as much undesirable experience as it has desirable experience. In fact, orthodox Christianity has had a habit of designating this life as a "vale of tears." A traditional way to account for this experience has been to postulate also a great malevolence or "devil." It may occur to persons having this pattern of thinking that the fulfillment of seeming possibilities for humanity, no matter how promising, would be constantly thwarted by such malevolence. Even where such a conviction does not rise to clear consciousness, there may be a feeling that human purposefulness is doomed to failure. Recognition of the absence of evidence of benevolent dictation of the general course of human destiny seems to carry with it recognition of similar absence of evidence of any malevolent purpose blocking the path of man's progress.

XI IS THERE A TIME LIMIT TO THE HUMAN ADVENTURE?

WE DO NOT KNOW whether there is a time limit to the fulfillment of human possibilities. If any should appear it may seem probable that it would be man-made. But to assume that there is none might be rash. If there should be a limit to the time man has available for putting his house in order to qualify for survival and for the best achievement, then how you and I live may have something to do with whether our particular people or our species meets the deadline, and whether the success achieved is of the highest possible order.

Because so relatively few people make the most of their lives, for even very ordinary people to do so may have significant results. How we live may have a bearing on the possibility of success, on the time required, and on the degree and quality of the success achieved. Those possibilities, it seems to me, are not something dreamy or just theoretical. They depend on you and me, on how we live today and tomorrow, on whether in our attitudes and in each of our acts we are increasing the prospect of the human adventure. The same undisciplined type of personality which would scorn the idea of a time limit for man's mastery of his destiny and will not undertake self-discipline, if an obvious time limit should seem to appear would shout frantically for extreme emergency action, on the ground that there is no time left for the slow process of building strong foundations for human security. They will say, "If humanity is at the supreme crisis— say from threat of atomic war—and is in danger of perishing or shrinking to savagery, why give attention to the slow process of character building? When the house is on fire do we take time to teach the children manners?"

117

Crisis as an excuse for not mastering ourselves is as old as the human race. The atomic alibi is but its latest form. To assume crisis and need for extreme emergency action always has been an excuse for evading the basic process of civilization: the mastering, developing and refining of our own lives and our intimate social relationships. Were the present alibi to disappear, another would soon be found.

The way to social usefulness has not changed. Public policy and private character influence each other. There is no source of public policy except personal character. Sometimes public policy represents the character of a dominant person or a small group. More often it represents the general level of a people. Within the legal or party framework, a government official acts according to his own personal character pattern. Legislation tends to fail which calls for a higher level of character than that which generally prevails. The prohibition amendment was flouted and then rescinded. Fifty years of antitrust legislation scarcely checked industrial consolidation. Miracles of social progress do not happen. Every step must be paid for in advance by building the qualities of individual personality which will sustain a better social order. The atomic age will not change that fact.

A holocaust seldom destroys a people. A great social advance in England followed the loss of a third of the population by the Black Death. The Thirty Years War halved the German people and impoverished the rest, but did not kill the culture. A century ago Finland lost a third of her people by war and famine, but there followed the greatest cultural upsurge in her history. Rome destroyed only a decadent Carthage. Genghis Khan delivered only the coup de grace to a dying culture at Bagdad. Those decadent peoples in preparing against crises neglected the foundation of national strength—personal character.

Within a few years each of us will be off the stage, atomic war or no. What counts is the perpetuity of a culture. While

118

we should not fail to deal with national and international issues, yet, except as we can be genuinely useful, we should not squander our personal resources in emotional disturbance over world affairs. The main job for each of us is to put his personal life in order, enlarging, refining and strengthening his personal character. In doing this he will of course be dealing with social issues and relationships.

Prominent Americans have hysterically pictured sudden death by atomic warfare destroying America. They may infect us with hysteria, but their real purpose fails, for after hysteria comes indifference, even to prospects of atomic bombs. The fixing of attention on crisis diverts us from the main work of life where the causes and cure of crises lie, which are directly within the range of our efforts.

Personal character determines the texture of our common life, and that texture and quality is the chief determiner of public policy. The compact to outlaw war as an instrument of national policy, which was adopted by all the great nations between the First and Second World Wars, illustrates this fact. Superficially it seemed like a brilliantly successful international achievement. But the level of personal character, with self-control, tolerance, good will, sensitiveness and considerateness, which would make it a success, did not exist. Such qualities are learned in the day-by-day intimate relations of man to man. They are not learned on a mass scale.

Suppose atomic warfare. If 50,000,000 should be killed, the population would only be back to World War I. If 100,-000,000 should be destroyed we should be back to about 1875, when the historian Turner wrote that America had reached the last frontier, and must now turn to intensive development. We should still be ahead of that period by the telephone, radio, electric power, electronics, highways, and modern technology. The findings of biology, genetics, and psychology would not be lost. A thousand libraries would remain. The scientific method would abide. Fields won from forests, and many engineering works, would survive. The population might be back to the present number in less than a century. However, if a breakdown should result, not from without but by a decay of character, decline might be as long-lasting as in ancient Egypt.

If there is a time limit on the issue of the human adventure it probably will be set by men, and not by outward circumstance. Now, during crisis, is the time to learn crisis manners.

XII DO THE PROCESSES OF NATURE DISCLOSE CONSCIOUS PURPOSE?

A PERSON trying to discover or to design purpose for his life must desire greatly to know whether his life, and all life, is part of a consciously designed plan. Considering the vast amount of writing on this subject, it may seem presumptuous to touch on it. However, for me to fail to indicate considerations which have entered into my forming an opinion would seem to leave an unjustifiable gap in this writing.

Man is a part of nature and subject to the laws and circumstances of nature. That, it seems to me, is a primary fact the recognition of which is necessary to clear thinking on the subject. But man is a unique part of nature. Can it be that, just as honesty is not a general practice of the animal world, but seems to be a gradually emerging ideal of man, so long-range purposefulness is something which man is adding to his biological life? In order to have an intelligent judgment of the matter it is desirable—more than that, it is necessary—that man should see his own efforts for purposefulness in the light of the ways of nature. This chapter is an effort to get close to an essential phase of man's search for purpose. I seem able to approach the subject best by referring to some of the ways of nature.

The methods of organic nature seem to be different from the purposeful actions of men. The principle of least action or minimum energy is considered to be one of the universal physical "laws." Inanimate nature, moving according to this principle of action, always takes the line of least resistance. Case by case, and instant by instant, the action of nature is that which at the instant requires the expenditure of less energy than any other possible course.

121

Least action is often or commonly considered from the standpoint of the total process involved, but the principle would seem to hold, also, for every instantaneous increment of that process. A ray of light on its way from the sun to the earth, or from above the earth to the bottom of a pool, does not take a straight course, but changes its direction according to the different densities of whatever it passes through, always taking the easiest or shortest course through that medium, regardless of where such a course takes it.[1] (As a case in point, put a pencil into three inches of water and note how the light takes a different direction in the water from that in the air, so that the pencil seems to be bent at the water surface. Physicists will say that this refraction illustrates the "principle of least action" of light.)

We might say that inanimate nature has no end or aim or policy, or that its policy exists only from instant to instant. Inanimate action is constantly being "pushed around" by circumstance. Where circumstance has considerable uniformity the successive instantaneous least actions accumulate to give the appearance of continuity of "policy." The reason why a river flows with some approach to uniformity is that the conditions of its movement are so nearly alike instant after instant that successive least actions are similar.

It is here that man, though a part of nature and a product of nature, seems to differ from inanimate nature, and largely

----

[1]Max Born, the physicist, wrote: "The real importance of the principle of minimum energy can scarcely be exaggerated." (*Nature*, March 4, 1939). However, an illustration he gave of its application to the movement of light is not clear. He wrote: "Light moves like a tired messenger boy who has to reach a definite destination and carefully chooses the shortest way possible." Perhaps a better analogy would be of a boy who starts toward a definite destination but repeatedly changes his direction to take the easiest way, regardless of where that course may take him, and finally arrives at a chance destination.

122

from lower forms of life. He does not always take the course of least resistance, at least so far as gross observation indicates.

The following example will indicate this difference. We might say that the "purpose" of a river, in always flowing downhill, is to reach the ocean. On the northwest coast of South America, where there are no barriers to cross, the few rivers plunge directly down from the Andes mountains to the sea, leaving thirsty deserts unwatered. But a river does not take the shortest course to the ocean if to do so it must climb over even a very small hill. In southern Brazil there is a range of hills close to the coast and parallel with it. Just on the land side of this range of hills is a river, more than two thousand feet above sea level. In some places the distance of the river from the ocean is only about twenty-five miles, but there is this ridge between them. At each instant the river takes the course of least resistance. In doing so it wanders far to the west, and then south, passing through country already well watered, and finally reaches the ocean after traveling more than a thousand miles.

Recently men with conscious purpose have dealt with that river. They drilled a hole through the hill, dropped the river two thousand feet, making it generate electric power, with the result that it reaches the ocean in about twenty-five miles. In doing this some men worked when they might have enjoyed leisure. Some Americans went to Brazil to direct the job when they might have preferred to stay at home among old friends. They went against immediate impulse, to achieve more distant ends. They did not, at least so far as obvious impulses are concerned, take the course of least action.

It seems that organic evolution, like inanimate nature, exhibits characteristics which suggest the course of least action. Biological evolution seems to constantly temporize, to meet the conditions of the moment with the least possible effort, regardless of the long-time results of such action. Some

123

people take exception to this opinion, though among biologists they seem to be constantly fewer. With the countless species and individuals that have lived, it would seem strange if nothing should develop with the appearance of conscious purpose. From time to time men have pointed out cases which have seemed to them to indicate that such purpose is at work.

It sometimes has been held that the fabulously complex structure of the human eye could not have evolved without the guidance of a pre-existing, consciously held plan. Yet it is now known that sensitiveness to light has originated in many ways in the course of animal evolution. It has developed on various parts of animal bodies, with a considerable variety of seeing devices, using different principles, some more useful than others. Some of these have been relatively crude, "blind alley" devices, from which the species involved never emerged into effective sight. The seeing devices of some species, which followed the same general type as the human eye, never got beyond primitive and relatively inefficient forms. Along the course of the evolution of sensitiveness to light there seem to have been random tendencies in many directions, with effective sight emerging very gradually from such variety, as acted on by natural selection. As compared with the eye of the condor, the human eye probably is very crude. According to Darwin, the great Helmholtz, foremost student of the human eye up to his time, remarked of the human eye that if an optician had sold him an instrument so carelessly made, he would have thought himself justified in returning it. Such is an end result of five hundred million years or more of evolution of the eye. It is the growing opinion of biologists that this does not supply any very effective argument for conscious design, but rather the contrary.

Darwin wrote of "the ocelli (round patches of color) on the wing feathers of the Argus pheasant, which are shaded in so wonderful a manner as to resemble balls lying loose within sockets." He describes in detail how the wonderfully pre-

124

cise and effective shading gives the impression of a spherical ball lying loosely on a gorgeously colored background, with the lights and shade of the feathers such as to give the impression of a real ball standing out from its background. He continued, "No one, I presume, will attribute the shading, which has excited the admiration of many experienced artists, to chance—to the fortuitous concourse of atoms of coloring matter. That these ornaments had been formed through the selection of many successive variations, not one of which was intended to produce the ball-and-socket effect, seems as incredible as that one of Raphael's Madonnas should have been formed by the selection of chance daubs of paint made by a long succession of young artists, not one of whom intended at first to draw the human figure."

Yet even here Darwin saw natural processes which seemed to account for such remarkable effects. In the course of sex selection, which he distinguished from "natural selection," gradually increasing elaborateness and precision of design in the male plumage went along with gradually increasing discrimination in the females they were intended to impress. Among the various species of peacocks and their near relatives Darwin found a range of development of ornamental plumage, from rather vague and crude markings to the elaborate and precise color design in the species of peacock we know, indicating that the development was a gradual evolution of design, guided by the similarly evolving esthetic sense of the female line. There is evidence that the female's discrimination as to the excellence of design in the male plumage has reached a remarkable stage of development.

Here, as with other forms of sex selection, nature seems sometimes unable to check a trend once started. As female taste in ornamentation becomes more and more demanding, with usually the most precisely marked and gorgeously decorated males being chosen, male decoration in some species becomes so massive and elaborate as to be a serious handicap in getting food and in escaping enemies.

125

In the numberless variations which have taken place in the course of evolution, there may have occurred numerous unusual instances which give superficial impression of having been consciously planned. I believe it is safe to say that fairly full acquaintance with even such exceptional cases leads to the conclusion that the most reasonable explanation does not call for the assumption that there is a conscious purpose in evolution.

In considering the possibility of benevolent, conscious purpose I think of the ancient, heavy load of deadly competition of individual against individual and of species against species. (This alongside of a vast amount of cooperation and other mutual aid, which also has survival value.) Often the competition, as in case of sexual selection, by its own momentum grows more and more intense to a point where the survival prospects of the species are interfered with.

I am reminded of how water runs out of a wash basin through the opening in the bottom. As drops of water press toward the opening they tend to push each other out of the way and thereby to set up a whorl. This whorl grows more and more until the movement of the water tends to "defeat its own purpose," and slows down the escape through the opening in the bottom of the basin. Ruthless sex competition, which leads the males of some species to tear each other to pieces, seems similarly to increase in intensity by its own selection, somewhat regardless of the welfare of the species.

I think of the vast extent of parasitic diseases which gradually sap the vigor and then take the lives of the hosts. I think of the excessive competition in fecundity, which makes certain that the lives of most animals shall be of insecurity, frustration and tragedy. If all living things were but half as fecund, the total number surviving would doubtless be just as great. This competition is somewhat like a group of people talking in a small room. If a few of them shout loudly, then all must shout to be heard. If all speak in moderate tones, then all can be heard at least as well. Nature's creatures in

126

their competition shout at the tops of their voices. I think of the extinction without survivors of probably much more than nine tenths of all the species that have existed, and of the loss of their accumulated racial experience.

Could an omniscient, omnipotent and benevolent purpose have relied so greatly on undesirable experience—pain, frustration, tragedy—for incentives? Undesirable experience is not just the result of man's bad behavior. As man emerged from his prehuman forebears he was not free and clean. He brought with him diseases of the distant past, as recorded in his fossil bones. These diseases did not begin with his immediate ancestors. The saurians of a hundred million years earlier had tumors and tuberculosis of the bones, pyorrhea of the teeth, and doubtless other diseases which left no marks on the fossil bones. Bacteria and other organisms have been evolving their methods of survival in the bodies of animals, somewhat regardless of whether they helped or harmed the lives they invaded. (Naturally, those which helped their hosts or were harmless would have somewhat better prospects for survival.)

It would seem that either the designer, if there be one, lacked compassion, or there is something in the nature of things which makes the experience of suffering necessary to the fulfillment of life. In that case the designer was not omnipotent. There were rules he must obey. Who made those rules?

The common theological course in the face of such realities is to say, "Mystery!" Having said that it is assumed that we can hold to the conventional faith, notwithstanding its incongruity. It seems to me that to use "mystery" in the manner in which it commonly is used to support conventional faith is dishonest. It appears to justify belief in spite of the evidence. It seems to me that the honest course is to say, and to think, "I do not know."

Nature seldom creates anything new. She tries to get over the immediate difficulty with the least possible adjustment. (I

127

should not need to repeat that when I personalize "nature" it is for convenience of expression, and not as attributing conscious action to natural processes.) Nature seems to operate by the law of least action. As natural selection continually takes the course of least effort to meet the exigency of the moment, seemingly oblivious to long-time ends, she seems to miss many great opportunities which conscious purpose might seize. How convenient if a man could grow new limbs when his are lost, as a lobster does, or fly like a bird, or be aware of obstacles in the dark like a bat, or hibernate in emergency like a bear!

Man undertakes to break free from servitude to the principle of least action, and to begin to determine his course by the principle of greatest value. To the limited extent that he has achieved human status he goes against the drift of things when that is necessary to achieve his ends.

Except as it is evident in man, and to a very limited degree in other animals, I conclude that I do not see evidence of conscious purpose in the course of animate or of inanimate nature. Some able scientists believe that they do see evidence of such purpose. I cannot conclude definitely that there is no such purpose. Such a conclusion would, I think, be justified only by a wisdom that is far greater than that possessed by men. I have refrained from accepting the classification of "Humanist" partly because of the tendency of some of those who use that designation to be "cocksure" that there is no purpose they do not see.

Possible Explanations of Man's Status. One of the commonest doctrines of the status of mankind is that we are here by the will of omniscient, omnipotent, benevolent design. Assuming that to be the case, the evidence seems to me to indicate the intent that man shall use the resources given him to work out his own design and purpose.

A second alternative doctrine is that whether there is design or no design, we are in a world of determinism in which, either by the fiat of deity or by the inexorable and all-inclusive course of cause and effect, all that can and will be is predetermined, or is determined by the nature of things, and that we are powerless, infinitesimal units in that determined course of events. As to whether that condition exists, opinion has been so conflicting throughout the ages that men never have been able to agree. I seem to observe an element of freedom. I choose—or am compelled by fate—to act on the hypothesis that a degree of freedom does exist. If I am mistaken in that assumption it is because it has been determined by deity or by the nature of things that I shall be deceived. In that case it may be that by compulsion I am taking the same course I would take if I were wise and free.

A third alternative doctrine is that purpose and design in the world are not mature, but are emerging, somewhat as human purpose is emerging. In that case our best course may well be to learn what we can of this emerging process, and to contribute to it as we can, possibly with a contribution that may be vital to its quality.

My wife for many years has suggested an elaboration of the second or third possibility. She says that to her the living world, so small in the universe, seems to be like a research laboratory for the development of "soul material." If white mice, hamsters, rats and dogs being used in a medical research laboratory could discuss their plight, they might express hopeless perplexity at the treatment they receive from the "gods" who determine their destiny. Some are intentionally and systematically driven to frustration; some are infected with disease; some are exceptionally well fed and cared for, while others from the same litters and with the same merits are starved or deficiently fed until they die from the results of that treatment. If the animals should discuss their situation they might comment on what seems to be an incongruous mixture of solicitous care and of ruthless distortion of life.

129

There is little free will among these animals. If the experimenters are humane and conscientious they make sure that every seeming abuse is one that is necessary in their research to discover important truths. Under a humane experimenter none of it is meaningless or capricious.

A similar explanation, my wife holds, would give life a quality of reasonableness. Perhaps a less than omniscient deity by exploration and research is seeking a good way of life. Perhaps the frustrations, defeats and evils men experience are but necessary items in that process. She says she sometimes has felt as though she might be a white rat in the cosmic laboratory.

A fourth possibility is that there is no purpose or design, and that man finds himself in a world where some factors favor and some disfavor his adventure. That is, he is in a world of "good and evil," with certain powers and resources for mastering that world and for creating and fulfilling design. In the almost unlimited range which design and fulfillment may take, it would be strange indeed if no pattern is possible which would make life worth while. The possibility seems rather that man will have difficulty in choosing between various possibilities of excellence, and that he will hesitate to commit himself quickly and exclusively to any one pattern, because of his hope that through continued search and development he can achieve design which is large enough, intelligent enough, nearly enough universal, and enough in accord with reality, to include all values. He will take joy in that search.

Are Survival and Increase Good in Themselves? That question may be on a par with the question, "Is it good for a river to flow downhill?" The river just does. So, survival and increase may be neither good nor not good in themselves. Like the flow of the water in the river, perhaps they just are. If I live along the river I may find it useful for carrying my boat to where I want to go. The river may have high

130

value to me if I know how to use it. If I do not know how to use it, and build my house on its bank, rather than on high ground, it may destroy me and my house in flood.

If I have built a dam and power plant on the river to generate electric current, the continued flow of the river is more than a convenience to my purpose, it is essential. If the river should cease to flow, my purpose in building the power plant would be nullified. Yet it would not necessarily follow that the river is good in itself. The value of the river to me is the value I give it through intelligent purposefulness.

Similarly, if man has over-all, long-range purpose for human life, then continuity of survival and posterity is essential to that purpose. If human survival should discontinue, then human purpose would be nullified, so far as we can know by objective evidence. But it does not necessarily follow that biological survival is purposeful in itself or good in itself. Like the flowing river, it may be purposeless in itself, yet essential to human purpose.

So it may be with the evolutionary process. There is much evidence that it is driving ahead, for seemingly about the same reason that a river flows downhill. Yet as man has intelligence and capacity for purpose he finds that this purpose can do for him what nature seems to lack intent to do. He can make the drive for survival and increase serve him to increase experiences that are good in themselves, and to decrease those that are undesirable in themselves, and to make life very greatly worth while.

If man concludes that this is his actual status, either by the over-all inherent nature of things, or by the design of a deity that has placed him here with freedom to work out his own salvation, then he can educate his interests and desires to that status, and can find sustained joy and hope in his adventure. Personally, as I have lived through several decades with this pattern of purpose, I have found interest in living to be strongly sustained, and to be a source of hope and joy.

131

XIII MEANS FOR NATURE ARE ENDS FOR MAN

IN DISCUSSING the nature of value I stated that, so far as I can see, the only values men know are experiences which to those who have them are better to have than not to have, or whatever helps to such experience. I stated that values vary in many ways, and that much of the wisdom of life consists in understanding the relative value of things, in choosing those that count for most in the total of living, and in shunning those that destroy greater values, and so cost more than they are worth.

With Nature, Desirable Experiences Are Means to Survival. If, merely for convenience, we refer to the observable processes of the natural world as "nature," without necessarily implying personality or conscious purpose, it seems that the aim of nature as to living things is survival and increase. Pleasure and pain, or happiness and unhappiness, if we may use those words as general names for desirable and undesirable experience, are to nature but means for survival and increase, and are not ends in themselves.[1] Nature seems not to care for pleasure or pain in themselves, nor to care whether it is pleasure or pain which man or her other creatures experience, except as such experiences help to realize her purpose. She uses pleasure and pain, one seemingly just as freely

---

[1] As to many forms of life we have no clear evidence of pleasure and pain or of comfort and discomfort, but only of attraction and repulsion. So far as we can judge with any degree of certainty, it may be only the higher forms of life which experience pleasure and pain as the human species does.

132

as the other; pleasure to lead her creatures to seek experiences which tend to survival and increase, and pain to cause her creatures to shun conditions which would threaten those ends. The geneticist, Dobzhansky, wrote: "The evolution of life has only one discernable goal, and that is life itself."

Most of nature's creatures, it would seem, do not have the power of reflective thinking which would enable them to realize that the experiences they seek do contribute to survival and increase. Probably a cow eats grass because it likes to eat grass, and not because it reflects that grass is nourishing. That is, so far as the cow knows, eating grass is perhaps an end in itself. Yet the likes and dislikes of animals generally relate directly to survival and increase. I do not make this as an absolute statement. One wonders whether it is purely for such ends that a mockingbird repeats the songs of its neighbors. In some minor degree higher animals sometimes break through nature's pattern and find desirable experience which does not relate to survival or increase. But substantially the statement that with nature desirable and undesirable experiences are means and not ends seems to hold good.

Not only does nature use pleasure and pain, not as ends in themselves but as means for her end of survival and increase, but in general she provides that her creatures shall not experience either pain or pleasure except as they are necessary to serve those ends. I use the qualification "in general" because nature's job is imperfectly done, and often she gets her signals mixed. Often her creatures feel pain, as in chronic disease, when it is no contribution to survival; and often pleasure signals are out of date or mistaken. For instance, horses, after being for a considerable period without fresh vegetation which they enjoy eating, will overeat in a clover patch, and so kill themselves. In the chapter on "Dilemma and Ethics" I have indicated the frequency of such maladjusted or mistaken impulses. Notwithstanding the im-

133

perfectness with which nature's incentives operate, in general in the course of nature pleasure and pain are experienced only so far as they serve nature's purposes of survival.

The continuing state which nature seems to call for in her creatures is that of neither pleasure nor pain, but of alert neutrality. Except as action is called for to serve her purposes, nature would have her creatures neither happy nor unhappy, but with attention unoccupied by pleasure or pain, and consequently receptive to catch any signal of danger to be guarded against, or any possibility of favorable opportunity to be seized. From nature's standpoint this is a desirable position. Either marked pain or pleasure absorbs attention so that it is less free to catch signals, and so may not be aware of dangers or of possibilities. Darwin observed that earthworms while mating are less alert to going underground at daybreak, and so are then more likely to be caught by birds. On the human scene we see many such cases. For instance, either courting or quarreling while driving an automobile is dangerous because in such cases attention is occupied when it should be free and ready to receive signals. I once ran through a red traffic light while listening to a Beethoven sonata over the automobile radio.

With Man, Desirable Experiences Become Ends in Themselves. While nature seems to be indifferent as to whether it is pain or pleasure which she uses to promote her ends, while all she seems to care for is survival and increase, and while happiness and unhappiness are to her only means to her ends, yet man does not accept that state of affairs. Desirable experience, which to nature is but a means to her ends, man takes to be the chief end of existence. Does any religion or philosophy picture other ends to be sought than decrease of experiences which to those having them it were better not to have than to have, and the increase of experiences which it is better to have than not to have? Of course, this aim calls for

134

continuity of existence, and to that extent the aims of nature and of man are one.

Man goes beyond nature. He wants pleasurable experience for its own sake, not just because it helps him to survive. To fulfill that desire he creates satisfactions, sometimes outside the ordinary range of nature, not because they contribute to survival, but because he likes them. Sometimes he plants gardens of flowers to look at, rather than vegetables for food. He composes music, not because it guides him to survival, but because he likes it. Instead of happiness being primarily a means for promoting survival and increase, as with nature, man reverses the process. With him, survival and increase are worth while because they are necessary to provide opportunity for desirable experience as an end in itself. Philosophy, religion and art emphasize this fact.

Since man *must* give attention to survival if he is to have experiences which are ends in themselves without relation to survival, he tries to arrange or to modify his necessary experiences so that while serving survival they will have an added increment of satisfaction for its own sake. His food is prepared, partly for nutrition, partly for his pleasure quite apart from its nutritive value. His clothes are partly for warmth and for sex appeal, but partly for sheer esthetic satisfaction, regardless of survival value. His architecture furnishes necessary shelter, but also satisfies a craving for beauty or impressiveness which has little or nothing to do with physical survival or increase. His house furnishings are similarly chosen. And so it goes through life. Man, while making concessions to necessity, also uses his necessary experiences as ends in themselves.

Men also tend frequently to treat their undesirable experiences, not as guides to necessary action, but as inconveniences to be removed by any possible means. When I have a headache, nature is telling me that something is wrong which needs attention. By taking an aspirin tablet I may re-

135

move the unpleasant experience without having removed the cause. If I am failing in what I undertake, nature may present the situation to me in a way which makes me uncomfortable. One course is to try to find the reason for the failure, and to try to find a way to surmount it. Another course is to "take a few drinks," and so to lose awareness of failure. If life is routine and a bore it may require my utmost effort, perhaps for years, to create conditions for vital adventure. But I can turn to gambling and easily get the emotion of adventure without the reality. In each case nature has provided an undesirable experience as an incentive for action that would favor survival; in each case mentioned, man takes easier action which he thinks will bring an end to the undesirable experience, but without taking a course which would favor survival.

The role which desirable and undesirable experience plays in the economy of nature, and the contrasting role which they have in the aspirations of men, constitute only a part of the problem of human purpose. Even if that part of the problem were solved, other parts would remain for solution. Yet, recognizing this as only one part of that problem, let us see what light a partial understanding of that part may throw on human purpose, and on ethics and religion.

The Nature of Happiness. It has puzzled me for a long time that writers in philosophy, religion and psychology have given so little attention to the nature of happiness. I use happiness as a near synonym for value, that is, experience which to those who have it is better to have than not to have. Other terms for desirable experience are felicity, bliss, beatitude, blessedness, ecstasy, rapture, joy, pleasure, satisfaction, gladness, fun. We use these words differently, partly because they are names for different kinds of desirable experience, and partly because of our personal emotional preferences. One person will give the highest place in his esteem to the word "joy," another to "felicity," another to "satisfaction," another

136

to "blessedness," etc. They all are used as names for experiences which those who have them feel it is better to have than not to have.

Happiness commonly is thought of and written about as a condition which, if achieved with wisdom, good motive and good fortune, may be held as a continuing state of being. Yet much of experience seems to refute such belief. By and large, when an experience of happiness has served nature's purpose it does not continue, but fades away, leaving a state of neutrality, or readiness to receive other signals. As I stand on the street and watch a hundred people go by I would judge from appearances that some of them at the moment are experiencing a sense of happiness, while others are experiencing pain, grief or anxiety; but that most of them are neither noticeably happy nor unhappy. More intimate observation through the years sustains such casual impressions. I should judge that this emotional neutrality is the condition of a large part of humanity a large part of the time.

As a boy I was acquainted with certain very religious people who testified in prayer meeting week after week that as a result of their religious faith they were happy all the time. As I carefully observed these people day by day I thought I saw plain evidence of pain and anxiety, but often neither happiness nor unhappiness. I concluded that they had come to have a doctrine about themselves which did not accord with reality.

So very often happiness comes as a relief from unhappiness as to raise the question whether happiness and unhappiness may not be equal and opposite, like positive and negative electricity. One has a period of happiness on release from illness, poverty, fear, dread or pain. When these adverse conditions have been long absent—when one has wealth, health, security—these desirable conditions do not of themselves secure happiness. The physically and mentally fit person does not usually have his attention resting on his fitness. A prisoner, after living in a foul dungeon, on being released and coming out into the fresh spring air, feels that it is heavenly. A mountain farmer, in good health and living in the finest mountain air, commonly is largely unconscious of either, while he may be unhappy about the insects in his garden, or from failure to be elected to a local office.

Once when I was nineteen or twenty I was collecting lichens in the Colorado Rockies. Seeing what seemed to be a new species high up on a cliff, I climbed up to get it. When I was perhaps fifty feet from the bottom a rock I was holding on by came loose, and I began to fall. By good fortune I caught a handhold in another crevice, and then in what seemed to be a very long time, with a very narrow margin of chance, slowly and laboriously worked my way up to the top of the fairly high cliff. At some points there seemed to be no further chance to go up or down. When I finally reached the top and lay under a tree relaxing from the stress of the experience, I said to myself that if I am ever unhappy again I shall need only to recall how good it is to have solid, level ground under one's feet, in order to be happy.

After more than fifty years I can still get a fleeting sense of relief and happiness in thinking that I am not clinging to that cliff. Yet that formula for happiness has lost the potency it had immediately after the event. Is that not typical of life in general? Much of happiness is reaction from unhappiness, and usually it fades a fairly short time after its occasion is passed. Favorable conditions, such as having one's feet on level ground, when long and continuously experienced commonly cease to give a sense of desirable awareness. Probably few people think of listing that particular favorable circumstance when they sing:

> Count your many blessings,
> Name them one by one.

It may be that desirable experience is not necessarily the result of contrast to undesirable experience. Perhaps contrast in desirable experience is enough.

138

In addition to specific experiences of pain and pleasure there may be a sustained, continuing general sense of fitness for living, and of physical, mental and spiritual well-being, or a contrasting general sense of unfitness and of ill-being, quite independent of specific experiences of happiness or unhappiness. Inborn temperament and condition of health seem to conduce to the presence or absence of this condition. There seems to be sustained sense of joy in living, and appreciation of the opportunity for living, which some people carry with them through stress and sorrow. Some people whose lives are largely taken up with helping others in distress, and who therefore are much in the presence of unhappiness, nevertheless seem to maintain this spirit. The tendency of nature to maintain her creatures in a neutral state except where conditions call for action, may not be incompatible with a continuing sense of well-being, and such a sense, by creating a feeling of adequacy, may actually help to survival. If one's joy comes from commitment to the adventure of life as a whole, one may have a feeling, regardless of adverse circumstances, that life is worth while, and there may be an over-all affirmative attitude which has in it much of the element of happiness.

I have made these seemingly contrasting, if not conflicting, observations concerning happiness to indicate an area in which I do not see clearly, and in which, it seems to me, there has been an unusual amount of unquestioning credulity, among scientists as well as among religious men and philosophers. A continuing search for purpose should, I think, give more critical attention and reflection to the nature and the conditions of happiness.

XIV STRATEGY FOR SURVIVAL

AMONG markedly successful populations there is a constant tendency to increase the proportion of resources and experiences which are used as ends in themselves, rather than as means for survival. Yet, for the sake of safety man must not depart too far from nature's way of using pleasure and pain, not as ends in themselves, but as guides.

Organic life, we repeat, is extremely prolific. No sooner does a society or an individual begin to apportion a considerable part of its time and resources to experiences as ends in themselves than it may find itself in life-and-death conflict with hardy species or societies or families or individuals that are willing to give up present satisfactions in order to get a firm foothold on life.

Favored groups have varied ways for trying to prevent or to mitigate such competition. They organize society in favor of the existing interests as against emerging interests—the "haves" against the "have-nots." Professions and crafts call for licensing laws, presumably, and often actually, to protect the public from incompetent service, but also with a strong element of desire to restrict competition. Peoples fortunately placed, as we are in the United States, build immigration laws to keep out others, though we or our forebears came for the same reasons that would lead others to come now. We build tariff walls to make life less competitive. Whether it is the haves or the have-nots which hold the ethically stronger position will be decided in one way by the haves, and in another way by the have-nots. Americans feel virtuous in protecting our workers from competition with the low living standards of the Orient or of Europe.

Our country has reached a state of prosperity where no small part of the experiences of life can be ends in them-

140

selves. But a fecund and hungry world looks at us enviously, willing to forego experience which is good for its own sake in order to get a foothold for living. For instance, we are proud of the good care we take of our soldiers. They deserve, and they have, human comforts as well as sheer necessities. In the Korean war one American soldier at the front was supplied by eight men behind the lines, including comedians and Hollywood stars for entertainers. Chinese soldiers, we are informed, living with great austerity and ruggedness, had only two men behind the lines to supply one man at the front.

This situation is typical of the world we live in. Always there are some, with strong foothold and favored position, who increase the amount of experience which they consider to be good in itself without regard to its contribution to survival; and always there are others who are willing to forego experience which is an end in itself, and to limit themselves largely to experiences which contribute directly to survival. There being almost unlimited fecundity, as soon as any new species or society or family or individual that had been among the have-nots achieves what seems to be a secure position and begins to increase desirable experience for its own sake, it will find itself under pressure from other have-nots—just such pressure as it exercised in achieving its own degree of security.

It never is safe to let present experience of value so occupy attention that future value is endangered. While men are enjoying present experience, or are cleverly muting out undesirable experience, they need always to be on the alert that concern for the present good does not menace survival and the long-time good. This necessity for keeping present desirable experience in harmony with survival is ever-present, and constitutes one of the major problems of existence. That problem is not the invention of pious men, but one of the hard realities of life, which we ignore at our peril. No life purpose, no ethical system, no religion, which fails to deal with this subject in accord with the nature of things can be

141

adequate. Ethics and morals are ways men have worked out in stumbling and imperfect dealings with it.

Man in his choice of desirable experiences as ends in themselves can take a very general lesson from a wild bird. As we watch almost any wild bird feeding on the ground we see it feed for a fraction of a minute, and then stop and look all about to see whether there is danger near by. Any family line of birds that did not take that precaution would soon be eliminated by hawks, cats or other animals.

Desire Can Be Educated. It is one of the great and encouraging facts of life that one's aspirations and desires are not given to him irrevocably, like the color of his eyes. They are subject to modifications, education and re-education, and re-educated aspirations and desires may be more in line with reality and more satisfying than those he had formerly acquired from instinct and environment. We can by inquiry discover what kinds of satisfactions will most contribute to nature's ends of survival and increase, and at the same time be good in themselves, and then we can train ourselves to find our satisfactions in such experiences.

Take a very obvious case, that of food. By competent inquiry we can find what foods are most suitable in the interest of health and vigor, what kinds can be produced most economically and so put the least burden on society and on the consumer for their production. We can learn to choose among such foods those that most fully combine maximum food value with desirable appearance and flavor. Then we can learn to prepare such food attractively, and can train our tastes to accept and to enjoy it and also not to be too dependent on the pleasures of eating. In such ways we can greatly narrow the conflict between experience which serves the purpose of survival and that which is an end in itself.

Such policy and practice of appraisal and selection can run all through life. The houses we live in, instead of being monuments to the fine arts, may be primarily functional,

142

fitted to effectiveness and economy of living. Then, with a minimum of sacrifice of that economy and effectiveness, they can be so treated as to be esthetically satisfying. As to house furnishings, instead of having many "objects of art" about the house, the minimum necessary fittings, including kitchen utensils, may each combine utility and beauty. A vegetable garden may be a thing of beauty as well as a source of food. In short, if men can overcome the feeling that beauty needs to be independent of utility, and that art must be chiefly for art's sake, rather than as a manner of dealing with utility, our lives might be far less encumbered and far better fitted to nature's end of survival, and yet even more beautiful. We then need to absorb less of the resources of life, leaving more of them available to others. We can train ourselves to find beauty and satisfaction in the way in which we do the necessary day's work, rather than by treating work as hateful drudgery, to be escaped from to activities that are satisfying solely or chiefly as ends for themselves. In short, satisfactory experience may be found in the way we do those things that are necessary or useful to survival. We may teach ourselves to enjoy doing what is useful instead of seeking satisfaction in nonuseful activity. This quite revolutionary change of attitude is more and more being taken. Half a century ago many well-to-do men and women in Europe, and some in America, were "persons of leisure." Such a way of living is now generally frowned upon in America.

The spread of this attitude will not mean the end of great art. Unless the long record of human culture is misleading, spontaneous creation of beauty will continue, and its best products will be highly prized.

Mutations and the Strategy of Survival. At this point in our consideration of the strategy of survival, in a world where nature uses satisfactions as means for survival while men desire satisfactions as ends in themselves, I wish to com-

143

ment on the part which mutations play in the process of survival and improvement. At first thought this may seem like the interjection of a new and unrelated subject. However, it is very near the heart of the issue under discussion. An intelligent attitude toward human mutations will influence our ideas as to health, morals, religion, statesmanship, and our strategy for survival. I repeat, because man is an animal and is subject to the laws and conditions governing animal life, we need continually to understand man as an animal in our efforts to deal wisely with human affairs. Therefore I suggest that the reader take the trouble to read this further comment in the field of human biology.

It is the nearly unanimous opinion of geneticists that the human species, like all species of plants and animals, is subject to "mutations," that is, to abrupt changes in hereditary character. These changes may be so slight or so hidden that they cannot be observed, or they may be so great and so adverse as to be "lethal," that is, they may cause the death of the offspring. They are understood to be random, that is, the change in the germ plasm may be of any kind, and may be beneficial or harmful or neither. Some mutations are believed to be caused by cosmic rays striking the germ cells and making changes in them, after which the changed structure continues generation after generation. There doubtless are other causes of natural mutations that are not understood.

In the laboratory, mutations can be caused by bombarding an animal with X-rays or other radiation, or by application of chemicals, and sometimes by heat. In a vast number of experiments with fruit flies (Drosophila), chosen for experiment because there is a new generation every ten days, a large number of mutations have been produced by bombardment with X-rays and have been studied. Mutations also have been similarly artificially produced in some mammals.

The greatest danger of hydrogen bomb warfare probably would not be the large number of persons killed or injured directly, but the excess of mutations which would be caused

144

by discharging into the atmosphere a large amount of radiation which might last for long periods, perhaps causing so many and such serious mutations that the human race would be vastly injured. The changes made in the germ plasm of any generation would continue through the generations. Such mutations probably would not be materially different from those which occur naturally, but might be many, many times more frequent.

An organism such as the human body is extremely complex and delicately adjusted. The chance that any random mutation will be beneficial is small. It is somewhat as though the works of a watch were bombarded by very small particles which would slightly bend or change the parts they should strike. Some such accidental changes would make the watch run better, but most of them would be harmful. So it seems to be with mutations in the germ plasm.

In view of the many mutations—most of them harmful—which are constantly taking place in the human species, what prevents its general deterioration? The answer is, so far as now known, fecundity and selection. In primitive human life, for instance, the birth rate generally is high. But primitive life is hard, rough and dangerous. Only perhaps one in three children born in a primitive society lives to mature and have a normal number of children. While there is much sheer accident and chance in the elimination which takes place, yet natural selection always is at work. The tougher, more fully developed, better adjusted child has a better chance to live. In this way harmful mutations tend steadily to be eliminated, and the occasionally desirable mutations are helps to survival. Personal choice enters powerfully into the situation. A person seeking a mate tends to select one of the seemingly more nearly perfect persons available.

These are fundamental processes of evolution. Without such continuing elimination of the less fit, the human species probably would steadily deteriorate through the accumulation of harmful mutations.

145

In highly civilized life this process of elimination of the less fit is interfered with. If all children are saved and have children, undesirable mutations are not eliminated, and there tends to be degeneration. Royal families generally are established by exceptionally able and vigorous men, and their children have special care; yet commonly royal families become effete, probably in part because there has not been enough selective elimination to remove the less fit members. During the past century there has been difficulty in European royalty to find royal vigor and stability into which to marry the heirs apparent.

A virile society probably cannot be maintained by having only about enough children to sustain the population and to have the desired increase; that probably would mean sure decadence. To maintain a sound, vigorous population there must be a considerable surplus of births, with steady elimination, so far as having many children is concerned, of those least fitted for transmitting a good inheritance. This is the seemingly hard condition imposed by nature. How the problem is solved will to a considerable degree determine whether in general a society will grow stronger and more vigorous, or will deteriorate. The problem is at the heart of a strategy for survival.

As we have already stated, men are always trying to shield themselves and their families from the rigors of selection. They establish family estates so that their children will be protected. They create favored social classes.

Such protection is not always bad. Sometimes, as when selection in society as a whole is largely on the basis of brute force or cunning, the protection afforded may create a climate in which finer traits may grow. Shakespeare or Isaac Newton or Einstein or Helmholtz might not have survived in the jungle. Mankind often profits by the survival of other than jungle qualities.

Yet, almost the surest way for a society to practice mass suicide is to create and to maintain shelter from biological selection. The surest way to insure survival and improvement is to accept the full impact of selection, taking care that such selection is discriminating, so as not to overlook a Shakespeare or an Einstein or a Saint Francis; and that it is free from caprice, accident and other arbitrariness, and is governed by good will, intelligence and impartially applied skill.

Eugenics in the Strategy for Survival. There are four major lines of possibilities for promoting human survival and progress. They are (1) the mastery of the physical world; (2) education, or the increase of knowledge and understanding; (3) the refinement, enlargement and strengthening of purpose and attitude, largely by the contagion of association with desirable quality; and (4) eugenics, the science which deals with influences which improve the inborn qualities of men. Development along each of these lines is essential to human welfare and progress. To hold that any one of these is beyond human ability or concern would be to largely surrender the possibility for fulfillment of human potentiality.

One of the most striking characteristics of humanity is that men undertake to tame the world. They domesticate plants and animals, they tame rivers, they are beginning to tame the climates in their houses, and are experimenting at taming the fall of rain. They undertake to tame their own inborn impulses. So must they tame human birth rates, and perhaps other elements of human reproduction. Taming need not mean suppression. There probably are more domestic cattle in the world today than there ever were wild ones on earth. There probably are more domestic dogs than there ever were wild wolves. A human birth rate controlled by informed and self-disciplined mores need be neither characteristically low nor characteristically high, but would be responsive to the existing conditions, and always would be concerned with quality.

147

For the maintenance of a stable and progressive society there must be more children born than would just replace their parents and provide the optimum increase in population. There must be constant preference of the more fit and constant elimination of the less fit from childbearing. Adverse mutations are a reality and must be taken into account, or loss in human quality will be progressive.

Under present or recent conditions much of the selection taking place is adverse. For instance, it was reported that from 1930 to 1940 the only part of the population of Chicago which had children enough to replace parents was that part which was on public relief. Quite generally in the recent past the better educated elements of the population have had fewer children than the less educated, the well-to-do had fewer children than the poor, those of high mentality fewer than those of moderately low mentality. Graduate students, commonly with good minds, generally postponed marriage, or at least having children, until about thirty, an age at which the general population already has had half its children. The fittest men have been chosen as soldiers, and the less physically fit left at home. If the soldiers are killed the population may be genetically poorer. Probably one of the most dysgenic customs has been for the abler, more vigorous and more purposeful young people to leave the small communities, where people more generally have large families, for the cities where in the past the birth rate has been altogether too low to replace the parents. (The present almost worldwide burst of births gives at least superficial evidence of change in urban birth rates.)

There is increasing social effort to rehabilitate the retarded, the defective and the delinquent, at the lower end of the genetic scale, and to return them to society where they may have homes and children. Medical science is becoming ever more skillful in saving the lives of weakly children, born with poor genetic constitutions, and in general in helping persons of poor physical inheritance to pass on that inheritance

148

to later generations. In such ways during the past century in America the rigor of biological selection has been somewhat reduced.

Conscious purpose is necessary to correct these adverse trends and to accelerate the freeing of humanity from genetic handicaps, whether they arise from recent mutations or from other causes. With intelligent skill such a result can be achieved without return to the calloused barbarity or ignorance of the past.

No population policy would be sound if it were based on the assumption that high birth rates will be a permanent characteristic of the human scene. Because of the necessity for surplus births in order to make provision for the elimination of the less fit, or for the absence of children on the part of those whose greatest service may lie in other directions, responsibility for parenthood should not be forgotten. A population policy, which is part of the problem of competition, should be so inclusive and adequate that it would be appropriate for a rapidly growing, a static or a declining population. For instance, if a period of atomic explosions should heavily taint the world atmosphere with harmful radiation, causing a great increase of unfavorable mutations, it might be good public policy to encourage a large increase in the birth rate, with corresponding rigorous elimination from childbearing of those individuals with the most seriously undesirable mutations.

There are some hereditary disabilities which are so serious and so definite as to justify public and private action to discourage or prevent the bearing of children by persons having those disabilities. Except for such clear cases it is doubtful whether as yet compulsory legal sterilization should be used.

Two occurrences impressed me with the need for caution and for substantial research in this field. I was one of the charter members of the American Eugenics Society, and looked forward to a course of responsible research, and to responsible and well grounded public education. The chief mover in originating the Society was Irving Fisher of Yale. He was a man of fertile imagination and of much initiative, but he somewhat lacked scientific discipline and caution. He chose as directing secretary of the Society a man who was an active propagandist, but who lacked scientific responsibility. This man embarked on a program of sensational and questionable propaganda which alienated most qualified geneticists and tended to mislead the public. After a quarter of a century that damage seems largely to be repaired, but the occurrence illustrated an undesirable possibility.

The other instance occurred during the prewar days of the Hitler regime. At a scientific meeting in this country I talked with a woman scientist who, as I recall, was in charge of the eugenics program in the Nazi administration. She was eloquent about the great acceleration of racial betterment which would follow the effort being initiated for eliminating the clearly unfit in the German Reich. The "eugenic" efforts of the Hitler regime developed into the poison gas chambers of Buchenwald and Belsen. Indifference to eugenic considerations would be no insurance that some future Hitler would not practice wholesale genocide in the furtherance of his ambitions, but the circumstance impressed me as to the danger of ill-considered eugenic propaganda and action.

Inept handling of human genetics has been more or less a characteristic of human history. Selection in the human species has been slow, erratic, often accidental or arbitrary, frequently dysgenic, often controlled by physical power or by aggression rather than by discriminating regard for over-all values. The existing degree of general ignorance and incompetence in this field is not necessary. In many respects men now have the necessary knowledge, or have access to the necessary knowledge, to guide selection in a way that will significantly speed the course of human evolution, and that without rash experiment which runs beyond mature and well-established judgment. Eugenic emphasis as an isolated concern may be dangerous. If disciplined and informed by a total

150

life philosophy which is based on free, objective inquiry and commitment to the common good, it can be a powerful instrument for human well-being.

Thomas Huxley, in his famous lecture, *Evolution and Ethics*, drew attention to the common experience that when men domesticate plants and animals, these domesticated or cultivated forms may do well under human care, but, because they have been sheltered from the rigors of natural selection, generally are not able to survive when they are returned to a "state of nature." He concluded that in a garden "where a state of nature should be replaced by a 'state of art'; where every plant and every lower animal should be adapted to human wants, they would perish if human supervision and protection were withdrawn."

That his appraisal was not entirely sound is illustrated by the fact that horses and cattle, after being under human management and protection in a "state of art" for two thousand years or more, when turned loose on the South American continent, and to a less extent in North America, throve greatly and multiplied mightily in a wild "state of nature." Also he failed to observe that the domesticated plant or animal was not simply "sheltered," but was greatly modified to suit human ends, which very modifications unfitted them to survive in a "state of nature."

Huxley carried his reasoning over into the realm of human living. He held that the action of love, sympathy, compassion—which provide the motivation for ethical conduct—constitutes a way for sheltering men from the rigors of "natural selection" in "a state of nature." Therefore, he reasoned, ethical living is contrary to "nature," since it shields men from the rigors of natural selection. His position was that "cosmic nature is no school of virtue, but the headquarters of the enemy of ethical nature. . . . The cosmos works through the lower nature of man, not for righteousness, but against it"; and that "Since law and morals are restraints upon the struggle for existence between men in society, the

151

ethical process is in opposition to the principle of the cosmic process, and tends to the suppression of the qualities best fitted for success in that struggle."

Reinforcing his argument he continued:

> Moralists of all ages and of all faiths, attending only to the relations of men toward one another in an ideal society, have agreed upon the "golden rule," "Do as you would be done by." In other words, let sympathy be your guide; put yourself in the place of the man toward whom your action is directed; and do to him as you would like to have done to yourself under the circumstances. . . . Strictly observed, the "golden rule" involves the negation of law by the refusal to put it in motion against law-breakers; and, as regards the external relations of a polity, it is to refuse to continue the struggle for existence.

This application of the "golden rule" seems naive. It is the very genius of intelligent ethics and morals that in the exercise of love, sympathy and compassion they take the course which, so far as can be seen, will be best for all concerned, present and future. That would be an unintelligent observance of the golden rule which would perform a service to one, and by the same act a disservice to many. Purposeful ethical action often must be in contrast to sentimental ethical action.

Huxley's pronouncement had considerable influence on the thinking of his day, seeming to justify the each-for-himself-and-the-devil-take-the-hindmost business philosophy which tended to prevail; and this influence still persists to some degree in economic life among men who may never have heard of Huxley. However, while there is considerable truth in what he wrote, his conclusions greatly overshot the mark, and are substantially misleading.

As to the "inherent" conflict between ethics and nature, which Huxley also took to be inescapable, his error resulted largely from two shortcomings. First, his imagination did not picture the great possible range of human purposefulness;

and second, the only ethics he seemed to have in mind were the emotional, sentimental ethics, not directed by intelligent purposefulness, which were prevalent in his day, as they are today.

Huxley confused what is usual with what is inherent or necessary. Civilized life can shelter men from the operation of natural selection, so that they become like hothouse roses, incapable of withstanding the competition of a "state of nature." But that is not the only possibility. Human intelligence and experience, motivated by love, compassion, sympathy and purposefulness, and thereby committed to the aim of making life worth while, can develop ethical principles, motives and methods which will serve that purpose and which yet will not reduce the capacity for survival of those who emerge from that process. Man is part of nature, and so his arts are also. Some species of "domesticated" aphids could not live without the ants that cultivate them, nor could the ants live without their aphids, yet we think of both as part of the "state of nature."

Ethical motive, when not informed and guided by intelligence and imagination, is inadequate as a guide, because it may determine a course of action in view of only a part, and often but a minor part, of the probable results of such action. A very simple comparison will indicate the difference between sympathy controlled only by emotion and that guided and informed by purpose and imagination.

I knew of a case where an undisciplined and sentimental mother would not allow her child's broken arm to be reset after a few days of unintentional neglect, because the process would be very painful to the child, and the mother in her active sympathy could not bear to see the child suffer the pain of the resetting. As a contrasting case, while a small boy, playing with a toy cannon I had devised, I got a discharge of gunpowder in my face which left hundreds of burned powder grains imbedded under the skin. My mother in her imagination saw me going through life with that dis-

153

figurement. She undertook to dig out the imbedded powder grains one by one with a needle. Each little operation was very painful, and I gave abundant evidence of that fact, but she persisted week after week until the last grain was removed. Many times she must have been weary of the suffering she was causing me.

Let us assume for the sake of illustration, what I have been informed is the case, that there is such a condition as congenital deafness. While emotional pity and compassion may incline us to desire that congenitally deaf persons may have good lives, including the bearing of children, even though such children probably would be deaf, yet if society has regard for the total social good it may conclude that the congenitally deaf should not have children. Such a decision may require the replacement of sentimental, emotional, but unpurposeful sympathy by sympathy which is informed and guided by intelligent purpose. But in a good society the manner in which purposefulness is exercised may need development in accord with both emotional and purposeful sympathy. In dealing with the congenitally deaf, purposefulness, sympathy, compassion and understanding should be exercised in a way to make possible the fullest, most interesting and most useful lives possible for those who in the interest of society do not have children.

The present state of conventional ethics is only moderately more advanced than were alchemy, astrology and medicine several centuries ago. Yet it is in the field of intelligent ethical purposefulness, more than perhaps anywhere else, that the fate of the world will be determined during the fairly immediate future. Disregard for ethical purposefulness is a major shortcoming. There is needed very substantial redefining and clarification of ethical principles and standards, and development of the most ethical ways of doing what is necessary. This is particularly true in the field of eugenics.

Contrary to the opinion of Thomas Huxley, intelligent, purposeful ethics will not lose sight of the necessity for maintaining the soundness, virility and excellence of the breed. Up to the present, conventional ethics has given but little thought to that end. To some extent prevailing ethics are subjective, uncritical, traditional, unscientific, and often dogmatic, based on claims of revelation.

Yet even so, Thomas Huxley's appraisal is inaccurate. Wherever civilized, ethical man comes into contact with the "state of nature," whether of wild animals or of savage men, it is he and not they who prevail. This is true, not only in case of organized societies of men, but also of solitary pioneers such as Daniel Boone and those others who first penetrated the wilderness. Civilization and some degree of ethical living have not necessarily softened mankind. Decadence has more often followed the decline of ethics. Today purposeful ethics calls for the courage and intelligent effort necessary to solve such problems as that of population. To what extent "the course of nature" will be ignored or combatted or cooperated with in human genetics will be a matter, not of any arbitrary dogma, but for intelligent judgment and experience.

✓ ✓ ✓

For the immediate future a large part of the promise of eugenics probably will lie in intelligent, informed voluntary action. The choosing of mates today in America is often a casual, haphazard process, determined by accidental proximity. Where college students in their assemblies are regularly seated in alphabetical order it generally will follow that some matches will result between those who regularly sit beside each other. Similarly, matches commonly occur between those who work in the same office or live in adjoining houses. Members of church congregations commonly mate within the home congregation.

Sensitiveness to eugenic considerations will lead young people to try to find mates with such genetic and cultural characteristics that their children will have at least as good chance at life as their parents. One of the nation's powerful

155

executives, speaking to an intimate friend about his worthless son said, "Why was I given such a creature for my heir?" A possible answer was that he had married a nitwit chorus girl because she was physically entertaining. That was only an extreme case of a course that is not rare. An informed sense of eugenic responsibility and of social responsibility would greatly accelerate desirable human evolution, both genetic and social.

Relatively little study has yet been made of the effects of different factors in human mating. Would it be desirable for exceptional native intelligence but less than average physical stamina to mate with exceptional physical excellence, though with but average intelligence? Seldom is a question as simple as that. Widespread cumulative studies of human experience might throw much light on such questions. Always there is the necessity for keeping the whole life picture in view, and for avoiding narrow technical specialization in human genetics. The social inheritance often is as important as the genetic, and here too, there is need for vastly more information than we possess. May intellectual and spiritual hybrids likely be stronger than pure lines? Should a highly spiritual mystic and introvert marry one of his or her own kind, or should they mate with a skeptical, practical extrovert? If there is mutual respect and tolerance in the parents, is it possible that the children of such a union may have better balanced personalities than in case each parent had married someone of their own kind?

Human genetics and human society are so intricately intermeshed, and each is so influenced by the other, that in practical life they cannot be treated separately. Yet to some degree they can be studied separately. While eugenics is a field in which men are largely ignorant, and in which ignorant action is dangerous, yet our present degree of ignorance is due in part to lack of interest and attention and not entirely to the absence of available useful knowledge. There are at present no impenetrable barriers in the way of a considerable

156

degree of reasonably effective eugenic choice. With a change of attitude which might develop as quickly as has appreciation of literacy, some degree of eugenic knowledge, interest and competent judgment may become as general, and as much assumed in education, as is literacy today.

Eugenic intelligence and concern need not nullify romantic love. Natural affection can operate as freely between persons who are genetically and culturally fit for each other as between persons who belong to the same social set or who attend the same school, or live on the same street, or who have similar bank accounts. One of the activities of eugenically alert persons would be the intentional broadening of acquaintance in order to enlarge the range of choice. Imaginativeness, inventiveness and initiative may accomplish much to that end. Recently a young friend of mine found herself in an environment in which the range of choice seemed quite inadequate. She deliberately appraised the situation, and two or three years later she married a man whose acquaintance she had made five thousand miles from her home.

With improved understanding and attitudes, the process of eugenic selection need not be tragic for those adversely affected. Many a person finds his chief opportunity to contribute to human welfare to be social and not genetic; that is, his contribution is in his work and life, rather than through his children. Nuns and monks and Catholic priests, and many and varied individuals have, in effect, reached that conclusion. For many persons concentration on one's work will make more distinctive contributions to cultural immortality than any which probably could be made through their physical descendants. This has been true of many of the world's great leaders. Personal tragedy need not be a general characteristic of a eugenics program.

The problem of world population may very profitably be approached from a eugenic standpoint. The control of immigration might well be based on genetic quality. Suppose that each country should commit itself to receive any persons who would rank in the upper third or upper quarter of the population of that country, excepting any subversives. Then quality would be free to move over the world. This would be a protection against violent aggression or invasion, for those who can go where they wish will have less need for revolt. A major interest of mankind, that of providing opportunity for the improvement of the human breed, would be furthered. As to the difficulty of rating merit, as great practical problems are resolved every day in other phases of practical life. Such a policy would not wholly solve the population question, but it would be a contribution to that end.

Various kinds of effective action in the field of genetics are now practically possible, some dealing with public policy in relation to clearly congenital defects, and perhaps some with population policy, as by setting up genetic qualifications in our immigration laws; but many more dealing with voluntary personal action growing out of what we may call informed eugenic conscience, or sense of responsibility for the genetic quality of human life. In the meantime, research and experience can throw increasing light on the facts and principles involved.

Given such sustained interest and inquiry, not only can some inherited diseases be largely eliminated, but strains exceptionally weak in body or mind can be largely excluded. Seriously adverse mutations probably will continue to occur, among superior as well as among ordinary families—especially if atomic radiation is not controlled—which in the interest of society will call for elimination. That will be a never ending job of eugenic maintenance.

Human genetics is so inherently complex, many of the factors are so obscure and elusive, and the underlying processes are so incompletely understood, as to tend to discourage expectation of effective control. During recent decades it has been common for some responsible geneticists to depreciate interest in eugenics as being too complex a subject

158

for intelligent application. Yet the future possibility of eugenic action is one of the great hopes of the race, and to avoid the field because of its complexity would be to surrender one of the chief of human resources. Man must direct his own biological evolution. Perhaps a layman in his estimate of possibilities should bow before the specialists. Yet sometimes the specialist is so absorbed with the immediate specific problem that his scientific eyes are not focused on the long-time view. Two small instances will illustrate.

In the late nineteen-twenties I had two interesting experiences. Visiting Thomas A. Edison, we were discussing the possibilities of television, which was then only an indefinite prospect. Edison said that he had considered the matter, and would advise any friend of his to keep out of that field. The complexity of the problem was so great and so unmanageable, he said, that he thought the final results of research in that field would be defeat. Also, during the same period, having heard of the theory of inter-atomic energy, I made some inquiry into its practical possibilities. A highly qualified and widely informed chemist summed up the situation as follows: That there is such a force as inter-atomic energy seems to be agreed upon by theoretical physicists. However, after considerable inquiry among competent physicists and chemists, he had found the general conclusion to be that so far as human control and use were concerned, such a source of energy probably was inherently out of reach and never would be available to man.

In the field of human genetics it seems not impossible that striking findings or developments may occur which will quite change the over-all prospect. For instance, pragmatic criteria might be found for estimating the over-all normality, vigor and vitality of individual spermatozoa, with the result that out of the many thousand present a few of the most promising would be used for fertilization. The time might come when the lack of such selection would seem almost criminal.

159

Eugenics is a subject which we do not need to know all about in order to apply it usefully. We now have more knowledge in that field than is being applied. In the very process of using the knowledge we have, the range of mastery may increase. Considering it one of the major keys to human advance, I see no reason for a pessimistic attitude.

I believe it is not unreasonable to look forward to a time in the not greatly distant future when the usual human being will be a person of sound bodily and mental constitution, without inherited disease or serious blight, and with what today would be called high mentality, with a good degree of temperamental stability, and with a general sense of physical and mental well-being. Eugenic consciousness and conduct will be an important element in a mature strategy for survival.

Pattern for Differential Survival. We may state a strategy for survival in general terms. Men can keep their wants simple. They can educate their tastes and desires so that they take pleasure in the design, fitness and quality of simplicity, rather than in multitude and elaborateness of possessions, especially of those which have no contribution to make to survival. Simple living and self-sustaining activity make less demand of the haves on the have-nots, reduce the element of competitive status, and in effect make the world favorable for a much greater proportion of the people to live with satisfaction and without frustration. This general policy of endeavoring to find satisfaction in living, while making minimum demands on whatever resources are limited and consumable, would greatly reduce the competitive pressures of life; there would be less conflict between nature's aim of using pleasure and pain as means for survival, and the human aim of desiring experience as good in itself.

Also, the general ethical principle, that opportunity should be made available in proportion to the ability and intent to use it for the good of society as a whole, would so revolutionize the process of competition in living as to make it an al-

160

most wholly beneficent process. A conventional religious expression of this principle is, "Thou shalt love thy neighbor as thyself."

If privilege and favoritism are eliminated, fortunate people will be sharing the lot of the not privileged, and will not grow soft. If the resources and opportunities of life are equally available to all who earn them, then there will not be a hungry mob beating at the doors of wealth and privilege, and there will be no doors of privilege to beat at. There will be no underprivileged ability, merit and vigor which will feel impelled to storm the castle in order to get a chance at life, and there will be no castle to storm. In short, men then would find their satisfactions in activities which would add to the total of social and economic resources, which would help keep them fit to survive, and which would tend to remove the occasion for arbitrary, violent aggression. Selection would tend to eliminate the inherently less fit individuals, and in a manner which would allow such persons to finish out their lives in ways which would give them any degree of cultural immortality of which they were capable.

Where there is no inequality of opportunity, there is better chance for the development of effective controls of population, since nearly all would be similarly affected by overpopulation. Conditions would be favorable for development of folkways characterized by stability, good will and fair play. It is the existence of such folkways that provides the tough stability of any society.

These may seem to be no more than vague, idealistic visions of a good society, yet they are such conditions as would constitute good strategy for survival for whatever had merit to justify survival. It is just such absence of arbitrariness in opportunity for survival which is the ideal of law, ethics and religion.

Beyond Unity. Should all the world come to be under one government, with an end of war and the disbandment of

161

armies, we might yet find major vital problems still unsolved. Prolific people would desire to expand into territories less densely populated. Other forms of competition might still persist, as when a religious hierarchy promotes high birth rates among its adherents as a way to gain ascendancy. The problem of the improvement of the race through eugenics would have to be faced. The question would still persist as to whether there should be any control of the over-all density of population. Should economic want be eliminated over the world, then the great problem would remain of how men would maintain interest in living in ways that would be personally and socially wholesome. For some of the most important of these problems society as yet has developed no clear standards of excellence and no ethical or religious codes.

Peace on earth and world unity in a political sense are highly essential steps, necessary to provide a foundation of social stability on which other issues can be worked out, but they will no more than clear the way for dealing with the deeply fundamental problems of mankind.

162

XV REGARD FOR OTHER
   SPECIES

I HAVE INDICATED LOYALTY to the human adventure as my aim and ruling incentive. However, I can see as my over-all incentive the fulfillment of the possibility of all life.

There are two reasons why one may favor the consideration of men for other species. The reason which it is most practicable to speak about is that other species may be of great actual use to man. It usually requires scores or hundreds of thousands of years for species to develop, and probably millions of years for types as different as genera to emerge. Once eliminated they are gone forever. With our present crude appraisals we do not know their long-time significance to us. One-celled algae (green slime) have long been a nuisance in many human situations. Water supply engineers and others would have been glad to eliminate them from the earth, and almost no one would have mourned their passing. Yet now we are told that the despised green slime algae have great and unsuspected ability to use sunlight to make protein food, and that under proper management they may become a chief resource for saving the world from starvation. We should be very slow in dismissing any organism as useless.

A considerable number of species have been exterminated by men. The passenger pigeon and the New England heath hen are conspicuous cases. Early man probably killed off the mammoth in hunting it for food, as he did also those giant birds, the five-hundred-pound moas and the half-ton elephant birds. Preserved and domesticated, they might have had a useful place in the human economy.

Our attitude toward other species has been similar to that we have had toward primitive peoples. In America, for instance, the aborigenes were considered as of little worth, and principally as obstacles to the pioneer. The doctrine that "The only good Indian is a dead Indian" prevailed even among "godly" men. In 1871, Francis C. Walker, then the United States Commissioner for Indian Affairs, wrote in his annual report: "When treating with savage men, as with savage beasts, no question of national honor can arise. Whether to fight, to run away, or to employ a ruse, is solely a matter of expediency." The "solemn treaties" of our government with the American Indians were sometimes treated as ruses, like traps to catch animals. This was true of some officials, though not of the American people.

Where humane considerations ruled, for the most part the American Indian was seen as an unfortunate creature without significant culture. Until recently it was the settled policy of "humane" administrators in our government to destroy the "worthless" Indian native culture and to replace it with our own "authentic" culture. There was almost total unawareness that each indigenous culture had unique qualities, some of them of great potential significance. They provided new ways for looking at life and value, and few things are so difficult to achieve or so precious as different outlooks that are the outgrowth of human experience. The rough-and-ready pioneers who made contact with Indian tribes were no more competent to understand the existence of philosophic values than would a common sailor landing in Boston be equipped to realize the significance of a nearby William James or A. N. Whitehead. Radin's *Primitive Man as Philosopher* gives a hint of qualities of thinking in the Indian of which the frontiersman was totally unaware. In destroying the social structure and the traditions of these peoples in philosophy, esthetics, and worldly wisdom, unaware that anything of value was being lost, we were somewhat like the barbarians who overthrew the culture of ancient Greece, burning priceless architecture and sculpture to make lime, and using paintings of the masters as surfaces for rolling dice.

164

Our own ignorant disregard for American Indian culture has continued almost up to the present, and as to social organization continues in current national legislation. This reference to the recent destruction of the values of other human cultures is to suggest that our disregard for the values of other species may be similarly blind. Psychologists are coming to recognize the existence of unique animal viewpoints. Our present contempt for the mental and personal potentialities of other species may be no more appropriate than the contempt in which we have held the minds of "savages."

The great long-time menace to human life is not atom bombs, but boredom. So long as the wolves of want and need are chasing us, we find life interesting. Given a universal economy of abundance, satiety would loom as the chief of all dangers, as is powerfully pictured in the book *Ecclesiastes*. Under such circumstances, every resource of variety and interest would be prized. Therefore, the varied outlooks of other species might become priceless resources.

ᕗ   ᕗ   ᕗ

My reason for anthropocentric emphasis in discussing the preservation of other species is the feeling that only from the standpoint of human interest can any large number of people be led quickly to take an effective interest in the subject. Loyalty to life as such is a quality not yet generally achieved. Yet there is a deeper reason for insuring that species are not eliminated. Man is at present so dominant and so egotistical that he thinks of himself as the only animal that has value in and for itself. He has treated all others as here simply for his convenience, or as nuisances to be got rid of. Just as his gods have been anthropomorphic, so has his world been anthropocentric. Man is now perfectly sure that he is the apex of creation, and that no other species is fit, or ever would be fit, to share his preeminence. This may be an immature judgment. Should man get outside of himself and get an objective view he might come to the conclusion that man is not the measure of all things, and that other species also have inherent value.

We are now superior and dominant, as dominant as the trilobites were for fifty million years. But some other species probably are as intelligent now as we were when we assumed dominance, and they doubtless are still evolving in intelligence. Without giving mystical or absolute meaning to the word "rights," is it not possible that other species also have rights to continue their participation in the adventure of living? Perhaps humanity is not unique in having rights, if by that term we mean potential ability to experience value which makes continuance of existence an asset to the total worth of living.

Albert Schweitzer in searching for a foundation principle for ethical living reached the conclusion that the underlying and unifying principle of all ethics is "reverence for life." Since he is probably the foremost living exponent of that concept, a few more quotations from his writings may indicate the meaning of his expression.

> The deeper we look into nature, the more we recognize that it is full of life, and the more profoundly we know that all life is a secret and that we are united with all life that is in nature. Man can no longer live his life for himself alone. We realize that all life is valuable and that we are united to all this life. From this knowledge comes our spiritual relation to the universe.

In the following profound remark Schweitzer indicates truly what in reality is the basis of all faith. Theologians and churchmen would have us believe that faith rests on acceptance of a sacred book or a revealed doctrine or on the authority of a church ruled by God's sole appointed deputies. Faith has far deeper roots than any of these. As Schweitzer states, it is an inherent quality of life itself. If the holy book and the revealed doctrine and God's sole appointed deputies all should disappear, faith would remain undiminished, ex-

166

cept as indoctrination had made it seem to depend on these other "foundations." Here are Schweitzer's words:

> Imaginative power, determined by ideals, is at work in all that is. The impulse toward perfection is innate in us—beings, as we are, endowed with freedom and capable of reflective, purposeful action—in such a way that we naturally aspire to raise ourselves and every portion of existence affected by our influence to the highest material and spiritual degree of value.
>
> We do not know how this aspiration came to be in us and how it has developed itself in us. It is an intrinsic part of our being. We must follow it if we will not be untrue to the secret will-to-live which is rooted in us.

Whatever the meaning to Schweitzer, the word "ideal," as here used, in my mind relates to that inner near-perfect pattern or type, whether of genus or species or individual, which the process of living tends—never with complete success—to bring to perfect expression. Each plant or animal develops, not in a random manner, but according to the type or "ideal" which is characteristic of its species and of itself. But we will continue with Schweitzer:

> Ethics is nothing else than reverence for life. Reverence for life affords me my fundamental principle of morality, namely, that good consists in maintaining, assisting and enhancing life, and that to destroy, to harm or to hinder life is evil. Affirmation of the world, that is to say, affirmation of the will-to-live which appears in phenomenal form all around me is only possible for me in that I give myself out for other life.

*   *   *

> Thought must strive to find a formula for the essential nature of the ethical. In so doing it is led to characterize ethics as self-devotion for the sake of life, motivated by reverence for life.

167

All vital religious feeling flows from reverence for life and for the necessity and for the need for ideals which is implicit in life. In reverence for life religious feeling lies before us in its most elemental and most profound form in which it is no longer involved in explanations of the objective world.

✶　　✶　　✶

Ordinary ethics seeks to find limits within the sphere of human life and relationships. But the absolute ethics of the will-to-live must reverence every form of life, seeking so far as possible to refrain from destroying any life, regardless of its particular type. It says of no instance of life, "This has no value." It cannot make any such exceptions, for it is built upon reverence for life as such.

✶　　✶　　✶

However seriously a man undertakes to abstain from killing and damaging, he cannot entirely avoid it. He is under the law of necessity which compels him to kill and to damage both with and without his knowledge. In many ways it may happen that by slavish adherence to the commandment not to kill, compassion is less served than by breaking it.

The principle of not killing and not harming must not aim at being independent, but must be the servant of, and subordinate to, compassion. It must therefore enter into practical discussion with reality. True reverence for morality is shown by readiness to face the difficulties contained in it.

✶　　✶　　✶

My main reason for keeping a rifle is to shoot the snakes, of which we have a great many in the grass around my house, and to kill the birds of prey that plunder the nests of the weaver birds in the palms in front of it.

168

REGARD FOR OTHER SPECIES

Though our approaches are somewhat different, I am at one with Schweitzer in holding that my over-all loyalty is not only to the human adventure, but to the adventure of life as a whole. Yet regard for other species should be informed and in accord with the nature of things. Sentimental affection without such control quickly reaches absurdity.

A pair of adult field mice, if they should breed and have a full brood, and if that process should continue unbroken for only a year or fifteen months, would result in over a million descendants of the original pair. Yet in a population which has reached stability there is room for only as many as at the beginning. The excess is taken care of by shrews, cats, birds, foxes, snakes, drowning, starvation, and the farmer's plow. Mice, and many other species, live in a world of enemies, danger, tragedy, frustration and death, and have a high reproduction rate which provides for such contingencies.

A man must of necessity husband his limited resources of pity, or they will turn sour or become morbid, but he should not suppress compassion. The Jains of India sometimes wear cloths over their mouths, lest in breathing they might inhale and injure insects. They were barred from farming because in turning the soil they would kill small creatures. So they took to trade. They are known as shrewd traders and hard bargainers, in some cases with willingness to live in wealth while their fellow men starve.

Regard for other species should be intelligently purposeful, rather than chiefly sentimental. The following attitudes seem to me to be reasonable.

I would not unnecessarily cause suffering to any animal. In research by the use of animals I would restrict inflicting pain to cases that are necessary.

I would relieve pain and tragedy as I meet it along the way, and would go out of my way to encourage humane treatment of animals in general.

I would have my sense of fellowship and compassion include other species as well as man.

169

I would be careful to preserve species, because I am not able to judge their value to life in general or to man.

Much supposed regard for animals is traditional or sacramental, rather than reasonable. In India many millions of nearly starved cattle roam the country, overgrazing and impoverishing the soil, preventing the growth of trees, destroying crops and living miserably. On an American farm the cattle are comparatively in heaven. They are fed adequately and carefully, with nutrition experts providing appropriate rations. Disease is systematically eliminated and veterinary doctors are available as needed. Natural enemies are exterminated. The cattle live probably as long as they would in a wild state among enemies. Then death comes mercifully and quickly. The chief misuse may be in overbreeding as for milk or beef, with the result that the individuals may have a sense of physical maladjustment. It is quite possible that more normal breeding would result in more wholesome food products.

There exists a sort of symbiosis between man and beast, which is generally a milder, more "humane" regime than that of wild nature. Schweitzer well says that reverence for life must "enter into practical discussion with reality" and must have "readiness to face the difficulties contained in it."

170

XVI THE PROBLEM OF
COMPETITION[1]

ALL LIVING NATURE is prolific, including man. Always a vast excess of life presses for its chance to live, to fulfill itself, and to multiply. This is one of the fundamental, all-pervading facts of life. Except as it is recognized, understood and adequately faced there can be no clear definition of purpose for men. The sentimental repudiation of competition, the holding that competition is bad, and that men ought not to compete, is wishful thinking and a running away from reality. On the other hand, the attitude that we live in a world of sheer competition, governed by the "law of tooth and claw," is surrender of the status of humanity and a reversion to the beasts, and to the less advanced of the beasts. If we can clearly understand the nature of competition we may see that it may be a good and essential element of human purpose.

What Is Competition? Almost no characteristic of life is more universal. Life may have originated on the earth many times, only to disappear because some element necessary to survival was lacking. To continue and become dominant, life must be adaptable to a great variety of conditions. It must be persistent, holding on in adverse circumstances until it can make adjustments. It must reproduce itself, or be ended by aging or accident. It must aggressively push out in all directions, or risk elimination by circumstances.

These are elemental characteristics which living things must have if they are to keep on living. But these very quali-

---

[1] In part reproduced from an article, "The Civilizing of Competition," in the magazine *Main Currents of Modern Thought,* March, 1951.

ties make competition, for in the process of multiplying, expanding, and overcoming obstacles it sometimes happens that the obstacle is another living thing, which also is trying to expand and occupy more territory. Effort to overcome such living obstacles we call competition. The process thus is as natural and inevitable as life itself.

In that process of expanding and overcoming obstacles, and of replacing losses of every kind, life has become exceedingly prolific. For example, consider a single one of the thousands of species which inhabit the sea. If every codfish egg should complete its life and reproduce itself without hindrance, and if that process should remain unbroken, within 20 years all the oceans of the earth would be solid codfish.

During the past century inventions and improved organization have made the lot of men less difficult, and the population of the whole earth has doubled. If every man and woman between the ages of 20 and 40 should have four children, and if their descendants without exception should do likewise, within about a thousand years there would be one person for every square foot of land on earth. If even a relatively few families for any reason have many children, their offspring, unless somehow eliminated, soon will replace those strains which tend to small families. Except for rare intervals, more life of most kinds has been propagated than can survive, and a process of elimination by competition has been inevitable. In the long run this has been true of men as of most other species.

Security never is complete. The aggressiveness necessary to give relative security for a species results in intense competition for the individual. The process never relaxes for long. When any favored species or person or nation rests on its oars and takes life easy, some less favored ones will challenge that ease, with readiness to work harder and to live on less. Ease and shelter from competition are forerunners of elimination, yet individuals and nations seek respite from competing. Men have largely eliminated the former deadly rivalry with other species, but against their fellowmen they still are hard at work trying to create charmed circles within which they shall be relatively free from competition. Men crave opportunity to expand and fulfill their lives to the utmost, like a tree in the open meadow, rather than to be closely and rigorously confined by the presence of others like trees in the forest. In such an effort a successful man may buy a private estate, where the crowd may not enter. Similarly, his financial resources serve to push back competition, and enable him to expand his personality, perhaps almost unhindered by the crowd. To secure such protection men and nations build walls, tariff barriers, immigration restrictions, and armament. They indoctrinate people's minds to accept their preferred status, and make laws and establish usages to the same end.

A man differs from the tree in the open meadow in that while the tree can spread its branches only a hundred feet or more, the craving of a man's spirit for expansion may know no limits. A Pharaoh could consume the life of a great nation to build a monument. Genghis Khan laid waste a continent and destroyed ancient civilizations to satisfy his pique.

Yet, the security which men crave never is completely realized. The less fortunate try to break through these walls; they disregard legislation; they ignore customs, codes, taboos. If birth control promises to solve the problem for one nation, then hungry and expansive peoples bring pressure from without, while within there is pressure from below. The crowd may storm the Bastille and behead the king. The great estates may be parceled out to peasants. The hereditary wealth of the English ruling class, buttressed from without by a great navy and by a myth of invulnerability, and at home by carefully indoctrinated servility, law and custom, may be challenged by hungry nations without, and by a labor party within.

Cooperative Competition. When the old shell of privilege breaks, and new men or new peoples have risen to power,

173

they in turn begin to repeat the process. So the wheel of competition turns again, and the law of tooth and claw or of the sword will continue to rule through the ages, except as some other principle or process enters into the course of events.

But a new principle has entered. It, too, like the principle of competition, can be illustrated from the world of plants and animals. It is probable that for long ages the only living things were one-celled organisms, each living its individual one-celled life, each fighting for itself alone. Then slowly there developed the process of associations of cells for mutual benefit. An account of that process would be the story of organic evolution. Of the billions of cells that compose a human body, each lives its own individual life, carefully separated from its neighbors by a cell wall, but carrying on constant communication and traffic with them. These cells unite to form tissues, and they into organs, each carefully separated from its neighbors, but cooperating with them. Finally they are united to form the human body, which has a life and purpose of its own.

This great cooperative of the human body strives to maintain an ideal environment for each cell. The cells thrive best when floating in a liquid bath, so each one is kept in a solution of remarkably uniform quality. The salinity of this liquid is kept nearly constant, and the balance between acidity and alkalinity is delicately, but powerfully, maintained. The temperature in health is kept within about one degree, whether in tropic summer or arctic winter. The turgidity or internal pressure, and the electric charge in each cell are controlled.

Almost never could one-celled creatures, each working for itself alone, achieve such perfect environment. Seldom has any dreamer pictured for man so perfect a utopia as has been achieved for the individual cells of the human body. If one-celled creatures, which live and fight for themselves alone, could philosophize, knowing nothing but their one-celled world, they might hold that the only sound philosophy is, "Each for himself, and the devil take the hindmost"; but the

174

course of organic evolution would give the lie to that doctrine. Supremacy has come, not chiefly by competition of individual cells with each other, but by replacement of competition by cooperation in living and working together as organisms. Yet the object of the great cooperatives of cells which we call plants and animals is not the total elimination of competition, but rather to make possible more effective competition on a larger scale.

Constant pressure for a place in the sun might be expected to lead men to rely on the law of tooth and claw. Repeatedly that attitude is adopted for a time, as in international affairs at the present moment. Yet mankind through the centuries on the whole becomes continually more orderly and restrained in his competition. This development is inevitable. Competition itself drives men to cooperation, good-will and mutual confidence, because groups in which there is internal unity are more effective in competition than single individuals, or groups in which there is internal conflict.

A family in which members live and work in unity will be better able to compete with the outside world than one in which strength and resources are consumed in internal friction. Similarly, the community or the nation within which the members most completely cooperate with and trust each other can best hold its own against the outside world. Competition between families, communities and nations inevitably drives men to increased cooperation and to mutual confidence within such groups. It may be said that, historically, cooperation is a direct development from competition, a way of displacing individual competition with more effective group competition. Just as cooperation might never have originated without competition, so also it becomes more and more true in human affairs that competition can be effective only as it is based on cooperation.

For a time cooperation may be secured by compulsion or by propagation of social myths, but such methods are vulnerable. People come to see through myths, and to rebel against force. Cooperation must be genuine and well grounded to last. The weakness of democracies today is not so much danger of external aggression as it is lack of internal justice and harmony.

A cynical realist like Mussolini was forced to a fundamental inconsistency. While he glorified force in external relations, his strength for exercising that force depended on internal cooperation, mutual confidence and good will. The term "Fascism" implies as much.

But now the question arose, what is external and what is internal? The answer of Mussolini was in the doctrine—or myth—of the uniqueness of nationality. Good will applies at home, and force and shrewdness abroad. But Italy was not strong enough to stand alone by the cynical doctrine of force. She must have allies, who have similar dependence on force and cunning, with similar myths of racial superiority. Then what becomes of the doctrine of force and cunning in international relationships? Is an ally but a convenience, to be betrayed when that is profitable? How far dare Italy go in making Germany invincible?

Thus the doctrine of force without morality begins to break down, even in international affairs. The same tendency is at work throughout the whole of society, from individuals, families, communities and nations, to societies of nations. In the long run, honor, good will and cooperation add strength. The cynical view adds weakness. Where does this principle find its limits? Not, I believe, until we have achieved "the parliament of man, the federation of the world."

Mutual confidence, expressed in cooperation, is not a tender growth which must hide in the crannies of the world, and be forever at the mercy of brute force; rather, cooperation and mutual confidence constitute the way by which in the very nature of things people must live if they are to compete with the outside world. Cynical force always may have power temporarily to take advantage of good will, and to have its way. Yet the seeming miracle does recur. Good will

176

and cooperation do take root. Cynical force is superseded by equity and order, for time and the very nature of human association favor their ascendancy. More and more human societies are coming to be like biological organisms in which work of individuals gains tremendously in power by specialization, but in which cooperation is imperative. The size of such cooperative units tends constantly to increase.

Cooperation does more than sum up the combined powers of those who cooperate. It multiplies those powers, sometimes to a vast extent. The energy generated in a modern power plant is much more than the combined energies of those who have taken any part in generating that power. The range of a telephone system is vastly greater than the combined range of the voices of its employees. In fact the two have no necessary relation.

These cases illustrate the fact that cooperation with specialization of work is not just a process of summing up powers. It is a creative process, bringing into existence powers and achievements far beyond the sum of the individual powers of the cooperators. Against genuinely, intelligently planned cooperation, individual action is relatively impotent. The larger the scale on which genuine and vital cooperation becomes established, the greater will be the creative increase. Yet cooperation to be most effective requires good will, mutual confidence, and unity of purpose. There is no equally sure foundation for sustained social power. Competition which rests on lack of mutual confidence and good will tends to eliminate itself.

In a highly developed cooperative society, diversity of effort would largely displace sheer competition. When a person has found the best place to use his highest abilities, quite generally it will be found that his work has some of the characteristics of uniqueness. It does not exactly compete with that of anyone else. It is filling a need never exactly filled before. It is adding to the variety and fullness of life. It is making more opportunities for others, rather than less. More

177

than a hundred and fifty million people are living in the United States on a far higher economic level than half a million were able to attain at the time of Columbus' visit. Effective specialization of effort, and intelligent increase in the variety of human activities, with a greater degree of mutual confidence and good will, have made the difference. The population now has more of the character of an organism, and less that of an aggregation of individuals. Literal "cut-throat" competition of Indian warfare has been almost eliminated.

What, then, is the place of competition in civilization? In an organized society the aim for individuals, communities or nations is not to destroy each other, but to find how best to justify and fulfill life by contributing to the general good. In such a society competition is not eliminated, but has a new purpose. Its use is to enable each person or group of persons to play the part for which it is the best person or group available. A man should seek to fill any place only when he is the best for that place, and when there is no greater need for him elsewhere.

In a well organized society, competition in finding and holding one's place is essential, and elimination of competition in this sense would be disastrous. The best man for any given place in society is best only by comparison with others who are available. Competition should be the process of exploration and appraisal by which each person or organization would discover its best work. It is the duty of the individual in society to compete. If he does not it is either because he has surrendered hope, or because he has sheltered himself in some privileged position and wants to avoid that measuring of himself which would lead to his taking his fair chance.

With this concept of competition as the process by which men and organizations of men find the places for which they are relatively best fitted, the ethics of civilized competition begin to emerge.

First of all the aim is not the special good of the individual or organization, but of society as a whole. The primary means of securing this end is the elimination of arbitrariness and caprice, such as in the past has so largely influenced the survival of men and of peoples. Chance and intrenched privilege must be displaced. Those who fill any place should do so solely because of innate excellence, and not by escape from competition by privilege or vested position. Those who fail should be persons or organizations without intrinsic merit. Failure should not result from relative lack of opportunity of any kind.

Next, success must be achieved by qualities which society respects, as good for society as a whole. There must be complete freedom of inquiry and open appraisals. All the cards must be on the table. Success must be achieved by honesty and not by deceit, by merit and not by favoritism—in short, by ethical means. The control and discipline of competition by ethical principles is fundamental to civilization.

No single social force should dominate society. It is when social forces are in right proportion and relation to each other that we have a vital and wholesome social order. There should be enough competition, but not too much. With too little competition there will be deterioration from lack of selection. With too much there is unnecessary tragedy of failure, competition tends to drop to ruthlessness, and discrimination suffers. Wherever men have presumed to be civilized they have endeavored, and with considerable success, to bring competition under control, to compel it to observe methods men can respect; but only at the peril of decadence have they tried wholly to eliminate it.

The problem of society is to speed up the process of civilizing competition. Our difficulties are due to imperfect vision of what constitutes a good society, and to the hangovers of instinct and of social habits from a more primitive day. For this process of acceleration to be successful there must be conscious control and design, and not unplanned drifting. There must be steady critical development of social aims. The doctrine, "Ye are members one of another"—that is, parts of

179

a social organism—cannot be realized fully except as a pattern of life emerges which will stand the test of critical appraisal, which has universality of range, and which will give optimum play to the human spirit. Hastily improvised or provincial patterns are like the bed of Procrustes. They require humanity to be mutilated to fit them. We must not hold any social or economic pattern as complete or adequate. It must have power to grow and change.

When we undertake to define the social pattern at which social policy should aim, we find questions of ultimate social value still unsettled. For instance, what density of population under present conditions promotes the highest social values? Is it fifty people per square mile, with great freedom of action and very large resources per capita, or is it a thousand persons to the square mile, with marked social regimentation, and perhaps with much less natural wealth per capita? We have no objective measure of the relative values of different densities of population, yet, as it relates to control of immigration and of the birth rate, this is an active issue.

Will the greatest social values come from equality in the distribution of wealth, or by distribution according to the usefulness of people to society, or on some other basis?

On such questions there will be honest differences of opinion. As a rule complex social issues are not solved by any simple, direct, logical process. Brilliant and far-reaching generalizations which seem to simplify and to solve great social issues, such as that "all men are created equal," generally turn out to be over-simplifications. The best adjusted organisms, biological or social, are complex and not simple. In approaching such problems some steps are clear to nearly everyone. We take those steps, and in doing so the next steps become clearer. In eugenics we have few misgivings when we prevent the reproduction of near idiots. In the distribution of wealth we are clear in preventing extremes due to great social injustice. In domestic and international relations there should be greater approach to equality of opportunity. We can stand

180

for fair play and not trickery, justice and not caprice, courtesy and not rudeness, good will and not hate. While we continue our search for ultimate social objectives we always find that there are relatively undisputed practical steps just ahead which we can take with assurance. In taking those steps the range of doubt becomes narrowed, and often the residual questions quite dissolve.

I think I do not err in assuming that, however diverse their views in philosophical and religious matters, most men are agreed that the proportion of good and evil in life may be very sensibly affected by human action. I never heard anybody doubt that the evil may thus be increased or diminished; and it would seem to follow that good must be similarly susceptible to addition or subtraction. Finally, to my knowledge, nobody professes to doubt that, so far as we possess a power of bettering things, it is our paramount duty to use it and to train all our intellect and energy to this supreme service of our kind.

THOMAS HUXLEY, in *Evolution and Ethics*

XVII   THE PROSPECT

THE SIGNIFICANCE OF LIFE. I do not know what the significance of life is, or that any significance is predetermined or "given" in the philosophic sense. I do not know whether there is any "God's purpose for the world," or any sure, definite, significant outcome for the world or for life. This uncertainty does not seem to me to be tragic or disappointing.

If there is a predetermined end, with the final results fixed and known from the beginning by an omniscient and omnipotent creator, then what is man but the creator's plaything? If there is no foreordained purpose and end, if purpose and possibility and end are emerging in the evolutionary process, then cannot man share in that process, and help give it purpose and direction and significance? This possibility appeals to me more than does the other, and seems not out of accord with the nature of things. If there is a God, then

182

perhaps he is emerging and growing, too, and man may share with him in the making of the future. If there is a predetermined plan by an omnipotent creator, then that plan seems to be that man shall work out his own salvation, and determine his own ends.

We speak of foreordained purpose in the creation as the plant is inherent in the seed. But we do not find complete finality in the seed, because radiation, or heat, or chemicals such as colchicine, may cause mutations in the growing seed. As human purpose grows from its seed, it is subject to change by man's objective inquiry and research, by his appraisals and his aspirations. Man's purpose and aspirations may create new elements in the pattern.

With the world of life the trend seems to be in the direction of constantly greater diversity rather than toward a single uniform type. I have often quoted Tennyson's

> One far-off, divine event
> Toward which the whole creation moves

as a typical statement of the conventional Christian view. Both that and the Marxian "inevitable socialism" seem to be unconscious carry-overs from the old theology. There seem to be evolutionary trends in many directions, with enlightened and sublimated human intelligence and aspiration as partly controlling factors in determining what trends shall dominate, so far as purposes for human life are concerned.

It seems a reasonable conclusion that among the apparently infinite possible trends which human life can take, some are more promising than others. In some cases trends are toward increase of consciousness, of sensitiveness, of self-direction, of control over external and internal circumstance. In man there seems to be a tendency, with many lapses, toward greater discrimination between better and worse. Often a gain seems to open the way to further gains. In the almost infinitely varied possibilities of direction of human evolution,

183

direction which is increasingly under man's control, does it not seem a reasonable prospect that out of this near infinity of possibilities man can find character and quality of living that will make the human adventure greatly worth while? What if there are endless possibilities of human life that are not worth while, just as there are endless ways of making a watch that will not keep time, and relatively few ways that will result in a dependable timepiece? It can be the business and the genius of man to discover what is worth while, and to so master the external world and himself as to bring into being a life that is inherently good. And what could be a more interesting undertaking? The very process of that endeavor can give great and valid interest to living.

Nor is it necessary or appropriate for man, looking at the unnumbered galaxies, to see himself as insignificant. If we consider only the mass of human bodies in relation to the mass of the earth, man is insignificant on his own small planet; and measured in that way, so is all life relatively insignificant. Yet we believe that man is not insignificant on the earth. In the long run there may be no need for limiting his significance to his home planet. His long-time significance may be without final spacial limitation unless along the way he meets competing significance.

The Prospect for Human Progress. The human race and its forebears have been running along for quite a long time, and it has not been an entirely happy process. Sometimes it seems that the whole of human history is a period of tragedy, with only occasional spots of sunshine along with the rain and the night. As we look back to prehistory and to paleontology we see that disease is far older than mankind.

As we consider such long-continued stress, such seemingly endless frustration of life purpose through the course of animal evolution, we see that much of life has been a denial of fulfillment. Man has struggled, has fallen, has been defeated, but also has had his victories. We see in human life

184

tremendous possibilities, possibilities of great refinement of understanding, of discrimination, of warm affection, of love of beauty; we see potentialities of excellence almost beyond imagination; we see in mankind a complexity of organization which makes untold harmonies possible, but also great disharmonies. Since life has such possibilities, it seems that the aim of life should be to remove the internal disharmonies which afflict it, to develop good relations among men and wise and good attitudes toward other life, and to surmount the adversities of external circumstance, all in order that the proportion of life which consists of experiences worth having shall increase, and that that which is made up of undesirable experiences shall decrease.

There may be continuous increase in desirable experience and decrease of undesirable experience. Desirable experience may develop finer quality. It may be more discriminating, keener, more unalloyed, more varied; giving greater range to personality and involving more of personality. Experience can be more secure, less subject to interruption, to disastrous ending. It can be more inclusive, covering greater territory, involving more people. It can be progressively more characteristic of human living. Increase of desirable experience in such ways would constitute human progress.

Several elements would enter into such advance in human experience. First we would list biological or genetic improvement. The geneticist Th. Dobzhansky wrote:

> Biology cannot fathom whether life may be a part of some cosmic design. But biology does show that the evolution of life on earth is governed by causes that can be understood by human reason. . . . It is a demonstrable fact that human biology and human culture are parts of a single system, unique and unprecedented in the history of life. Human evolution cannot be understood except as a result of interaction of biological and social variables. . . . Human genetics has not been superseded by human culture; the former remains the foundation which enables

185

man to manifest the kinds of behavior which are called social and cultural. An insight into the workings of the human genotype, and of the human gene pool, are indispensable for understanding man.

The interrelations between biology and culture are, however, reciprocal. Social life, and especially the development of civilizations, have influenced the evolutionary pattern of the human species so decisively that human biology is incomprehensible apart from the human frame of reference. The ancestors of the human species have gradually evolved a highly developed brain. The human brain proved to be an adaptive mechanism of matchless power and efficiency.

Within the general human pattern, man has the power to determine his own genetic constitution.

As to physical, mental and social hygiene, in view of present knowledge and the possibilities of research, it seems not unreasonable to expect that bodily and mental ailments due to ignorance and lack of care will largely disappear. Mental stresses due to superstition, false theology, warped folkways, and the socially inherited twists of mind from which people suffer, will disappear with the general extension of human sympathy, good will, the scientific temper, and freedom from mental coercion.

The mastery of the physical world, which for the whole duration of human life up to the past three or four centuries seemed beyond human reach, now has increasingly effective attention, and its lack no longer threatens to be a major barrier to keep men from the good life.

Ranking high among unsolved problems is that of the taming of power. The seeking and the exercise of irresponsible power has been one of the most grievous afflictions of the race. The permanent taming and harnessing of personal power should be near the top of the agenda of unfinished business. It probably will be less the result of frontal attack than an indirect result of the increase of personal courage, of insight, and of social commitment, which leaves little of credulity, of cowardice and of short-sighted self-interest for power to feed on.

There remains the mastery of man's own personality, character and motives. Strong men, wise men and powerful men are not necessarily good men. Just now we see how the greatly increased mastery of the physical world, which might be removing want from the earth, becomes a threat to man's very existence. Today even more important than better genetic strains, better physical health, or increased mastery of the physical world, is the clarification and refinement of human purpose, and the emotional commitment of men to live by the best they know.

There is a feeling abroad today that while men may rapidly gain ground in all these other respects, yet in personal character, motives and sincere commitment to the best they know, men are surely held back from progress, if not by a personal devil, then by inborn traits or by some pervading influence against which men and society are largely helpless. That attitude, I hold, is not based on the necessary nature of things, but on a state of mind which is socially and not genetically inherited.

There are several reasons for the prevailing lack of interest in the ethical and spiritual refinement of life, and in full emotional commitment to one's ethical and spiritual convictions. Ethical codes and standards have been the considered judgments of men as to how practical problems of conduct could best be handled. But they have been presented as authoritative dicta from men of competent judgment for the guidance of men who lack such judgment, and who therefore must be directed by authority. Very commonly ethical or moral rules have been presented as absolutes, revealed from above. In the moving about of populations which has occurred during the past few thousand years, men with fixed, revealed codes of conduct have been meeting other men with other fixed, revealed codes containing elements that are

187

different from their own. In the necessary adjustment the authority of such codes is weakened. Most moral codes are transmitted from generation to generation by the intimate relations of the members of human societies, including family, church and community. As these social groups disintegrate or are weakened, the traditional moral codes are weakened.

One of the chief reasons why desirable standards of behavior have not been more fully followed is that they have not seemed really important. They might be important for saving one's soul from a speculative hell, but for practical, everyday affairs ordinary custom seemed preferable, especially when such custom was in line with animal drives or direct personal interest. In the present-day western world this lack of a feeling of importance is increased by the fact that there are no generally accepted grounds for ethical conduct. To most people the prevailing folkways provide the chief authority. We often hear it said, "Everybody really knows what is right or wrong." In such case, "everybody" consists of those whose folkways are like our own. Religious authority is another most common basis for ethical opinion. With only a few people are ethics a matter of reasoned judgment.

The lower animals seem to live by impulse rather than by conscious purposefulness. In the human species conscious, reflective purposefulness has emerged gradually. It seems to be a characteristic of but a limited proportion of men, and then often to only a limited extent. Most men give to purposefulness but a small part of their potential energies, and spend much of their margin of leisure in getting life to pass in trivial pursuits and uncreative ways. Most of the world wastes a large part of its leisure. The person who uses all of his— and by use I would include needed relaxation and refreshment and experience of fellowship—can make headway with life, and usually can survive even when his exacting ethical standards are a handicap to quick material success.

One of the tragedies of life is the large number of people who have not found anything significant to do with their lives,

188

and who try to fill them with "busywork." This purposelessness is not due primarily to genetic limitation, but to the fact that many men have not yet become infected with the concept and spirit of conscious purposefulness. Contact with purposefulness and infection with purposefulness, especially in very early life, may steadily increase the proportion of men who undertake to give conscious direction and content to their lives.

There has been inadequate conviction that human conduct and motives are really of deep concern. But now a change is coming; partly through growing freedom from traditional authority, partly from increased education, partly from observation of the breakdown of a modern society in which personal action and motives deteriorate in the lack of a public opinion to support them; partly from the growing realization that with man's increasing control of nature he may destroy himself unless his motives are changed. Everywhere men are saying that science and technology have run ahead of character and motive. It seems possible that this growing realization may result in an awakening to the need of great change in human motives, incentives and ethical sensitiveness.

It is general lack of interest in the subject, and not any fundamental difficulty of inquiry in that field, which has prevented greater awareness of the need for ethical inquiry and development. The possibilities of science and technology were as great during the Middle Ages, when attention was centered on theology, crusades, and war, as they are today. What was lacking was interest in science and technology. The same is true today as to man's ethical and spiritual development. Men's interests are largely determined by tradition and by circumstance. Purposeful men can influence and change the existing currents of attention. Should the prevailing interest come to run as strongly in the direction of ethical and spiritual improvement as it now runs in the direction of mastery of the physical world, no less striking changes might

189

result. If men had been questioned a thousand years ago as to the relative possibilities of changing the personal attitudes of men, and of mastering the physical universe to such an extent that men could fly across the ocean, talk across a continent, eliminate disease, and carry vast power over wires; it is probable that, except where their minds were blocked by theological doctrines, the changing of men's purposes would have seemed the more feasible.

If the attention and expectation of men should be turned toward changing, refining, enlarging and informing men's purposes and incentives, it is probable that the changes which would occur in a century or so would be as great as those which have occurred during the past century in the mastery of the physical world. This may be the more true if there is acceptance of free critical inquiry, rather than demand for the acceptance of standards presented as sent down from heaven, the reasons for which are beyond the understanding of men. The refinement of human purpose is not a mysterious process, beyond understanding and depending on blind acceptance of authority. It is a feasible human enterprise, well within the scope of human ability. There are no insuperable barriers in human nature, or in the nature of things, which prevent such achievement.

The spirit of risk and of adventure may be more reasonably exercised in such adventure than in going on crusades to the Holy Land, in climbing Mount Everest, in trying to conquer people and to assemble a kingdom, or in trying to build an industrial empire. In all these fields men seek for significant experience at risk to themselves. In each one, most men are imitators. They follow the prevailing vogue, though with a little creative imagination they would see that the results to a large extent will be inherently sterile. Once let the imagination of men come to realize the great change in the human situation which would result from the intelligent, critically determined refinement of human purpose and motive, the trend of interest in that undertaking may well

190

develop at least as much attention as does scientific research, industrial pioneering, or political action.

Given such a trend of interest, the commitment of men's emotional loyalty to the refinement of purpose and incentive probably would have at least as great influence on the quality of human life as has science or technology. In looking ahead to the possibilities of human life it is not necessary to set limits in the field of human motives and purposes any more than in the mastery of the physical world.

It seems to me that there is one supreme virtue a man may have. It is loyalty to the adventure of life. If there is one supreme disloyalty, one greatest course of treason, possible to men, it is that in this great adventure, this struggle, this searching for a good way of life, we do not do the best we can. To be a dilettante, playing with life, is treason.

Playing with life as a dilettante has no relation to joy in living, nor to having suitable relaxation, enjoyment, leisure and pleasure along the way. If no one should practice at making music until all human troubles and risks are over, and until everyone had time to listen, then when that time should come there would be no great music to listen to, no musical tradition to inspire us. As we travel through life we must learn by experience where the values of living lie. We must learn about desirable experiences by having them. As to what constitutes purposeful living, great tolerance of judgment is appropriate. Darwin used his inherited economic position, resources and opportunity, which might properly be described as special privilege, for leisure to do his great work.

As we examine one by one what seem to be the chief barriers in the way of substantial and continuing human progress, none of them seems to be impassable. The chief obstacles seem to be in limitations of human culture as embedded in the minds of men. The rigidity of cultural patterns is growing less, and the comparing of varied life patterns is increasing. These are favorable signs.

191

BIBLIOGRAPHY

A list of publications referred to in the text; pages on which the reference is made are given after the citation.

The Major Features of Evolution, by George Gaylord Simpson (New York, Columbia University Press, 1953, xx, 434 pp.). Page 32.

Genetics and the Origin of Species, by Theo. G. Dobzhansky (New York, Columbia University Press, 3rd rev. ed., 1951, x, 364 pp.). Pages 40, 48, 133, 185.

Lives of Game Animals, by Ernest Thompson Seton, Vol. 3, section on "The Moose" (Garden City, N.Y., Doubleday, 1927, xiv, 780 pp.). Page 41.

Where Is Science Going? by Max Planck (New York, W. W. Norton Co., 1932, 221 pp.). Page 57.

Scientific Autobiography and Other Papers, by Max Planck (New York, Philosophical Library, 1949, 192 pp.). Pages 59-60.

The Genius of Solitude, by W. R. Alger (about 1880). Page 82.

Speaking of Man, by Abraham Myerson (New York, Knopf, 1950, vii, 279 pp.). Page 104.

Albert Schweitzer: An Anthology, edited by Charles R. Joy (Boston, Beacon Press, 1947, 323 pp.). Pages 113, 166.

The Frontier in American History, by Frederick Jackson Turner (New York, Henry Holt and Co., 1920, 375 pp.). Page 119.

Nature magazine, March 4, 1939 (article by Max Born). Page 122.

The Origin of Species, the Descent of Man, and Selection in Relation to Sex, by Charles Darwin (New York, The Modern Library, 1936, 1000 pages). Page 134.

Evolution and Ethics, and Other Essays, by Thomas H. Huxley (New York, D. Appleton and Co., 1896, xv, 334 pp.). Pages 152-53.

Primitive Man as Philosopher, by Paul Radin (New York, D. Appleton and Co., 1927, 402 pp.). Page 164.

INDEX

(See also the topical Table of Contents, which serves to supplement this Index.)

194

INDEX

Honey bees: avoid sex competition, 42n
Hope: should be based on actuality, 109
Human adventure: primary loyalty is to the, 108-109, 190-191
Human evolution: numberless variations possible, 183
Human right: defined, 84
Human selection: now tends to be adverse, 148-49
Huxley, Julian: science and value, 60
Huxley, Thomas: on nature vs. morals, 151-153; quote from "Evolution and Ethics," 182

Idealizing impulse: in field of values, 57
Ideal pattern: all life strives to achieve, 94
Incentives: man can remake his, 107
Incubator: the earth as, for human race, 103
India: effect of missions in, 70; results of speculative philosophy in, 97-98
"Inevitable socialism": carry-over from old theology, 183
Inquiry, free: a duty, 14-15

Jains of India: attitude toward animals, 169

Laboratory, cosmic: possible explanation of life, 129-30
Lake bed: subdivision of, example of tradition, 29-30
Least action: physical and biological principle, 121-123, 128; nature of, 122

Mankind: not necessarily inconsequential, 184

Marriage vows: undesirableness of, 85-86
Martyrs: seldom desired complete freedom, 17
Masonic order: members favored each other, 21-2
Moose: use of antlers, 41-2
Moral codes: origins and reasons for weakening of, 187
More, Thomas: condemned heretics, 17
Moslems: strongly orthodox, 13; method of proselyting, 70
Motivation: conflicting pressures to influence, 6
Mussolini: faced dilemma of cynicism, 176
Mutations: can be induced, 144; effects of, 145
Myerson, Dr. Abraham: on character affected by injury, 104

Nalanda: Buddhist university at, 99
Nature: seldom creates anything new, 127

Opium: not desirable to test, 28; a transient value, 55
"Original sin": biological interpretation of, 50
Other species: desirable attitudes toward, 169

Paganism: of Africa, and modern miracle religion, 73
Patriotism: origin and nature of, 49
Peace and unity: but clear way for fundamental problems, 162
Physical disaster: growing protection from, 100
Physical mastery: an American obsession, 105

195